UNLEASHED

AND

UNAFRAID

Courageous Women Transforming Generations Through the Excellence of Leadership

Volume II

DR. SABRENA DAVIS

Author, Speaker, Minister & Educator

www.drsabrenadavis.com

UNLEASHED AND UNAFRAID – VOLUME II

© 2018 by Dr. Sabrena Davis

Published by Dr. Sabrena Davis

P.O. Box 16422

Chicago, IL 60616

www.drsabrenadavis.com

ISBN: 978-0-692-17594-1

Printed in the United States of America

Library of Congress Number 1-6876194591

All rights reserved. No part of this publication shall be reproduced, stored in a retrieval system, or transmitted in any form or by any means, electronic or mechanical, including electronic, photocopy, recording, etc. without the written permission of the author, except for the inclusion of brief quotations in printed reviews, interviews or publicity.

Unless otherwise indicated, Scripture quotations embedded in the manuscript are from the Holy Bible, King James Version.

Scripture quotations preceding each chapter are from the Holy Bible, New International Version.

Cover design by Shirri Buchanan | Flaming Sword Productions
www.flamingswordproductions.org
e: flamingswordwitty@gmail.com

DEDICATION

This book is dedicated to

Every woman who dares to take the courage to lead her life intentionally!

Every woman who desires to grow her leadership in meaningful ways that impact current and future generations!

Every woman who renounces fear and walks by faith!

Every girl who dreams of changing the world and attempts to do it!

Every woman who is making a comeback by reclaiming the reins of your life!

Every woman who is reproducing herself by training and supporting other women in leadership!

Every woman who is intentionally building a legacy while leading others to greatness!

Every woman who is passionately serving as conduits, employers, mentors and coaches!

Every woman who gives a voice to others and teaches others how to sustain their life and leadership!

Every woman of integrity who openly models honesty, diligence, patience, perseverance, hope, justice, wisdom and humility!

Every woman who serves as light and salt in the earth!

Every Unleashed And Unafraid woman of the past, present and future!

Every woman who challenges the status quo and shows up in the fight of life prepared to lead through excellence!

THANK YOU

To Daddy God

For choosing and using me to lead this incredible Unleashed And Unafraid Movement that is literally transforming the lives of people across the globe.

My husband, Theo Davis

For your love, support and continuous belief in my creatively wild and innovative work. I decree blessings and favor over your life as you lead our family and others to greatness. May you prosper in every good way!

The Featured Women of Unleashed And Unafraid

For trusting the God in me to share a snippet of your story to inspire, empower, teach, and transform generations. Your leadership impact is astounding. Keep Soaring!

My Mother, Dr. Brenda L. Peterson

For being my first teacher, leader and model example of a courageous woman who leads by faith. You are a creative genius whom I love, respect and admire. May God grant you the desires of your heart as you continue to live Unleashed And Unafraid.

My Pastors, Apostle John & Prophetess Rosemary Abercrombie

For your leadership, revelatory teaching, training, and love. Your mentorship has catapulted me in a myriad of ways. Thank you for setting the stage and introducing me to the global ministry community in Africa and beyond.

My Unleashed And Unafraid Sisters, Friends & Supporters

For reading the book and joining the Movement! I appreciate you more than you will ever know. Thank you for every book purchase, conference registration, webinar engagement, word of encouragement, and positive prayer. Keep being light and salt!

My Cover Designer, Lady Shirri Buchanan

For your creative genius, publishing expertise, and excellent service. You are a true gem. May your gift continuously bring you before great men across the globe. Keep leading the way and modeling excellence.

My Sponsor, Panish & Boyle LLP

For your support, sponsorship and legal leadership. May your firm continue to flourish and prosper. I respect and greatly admire your transformational work. Keep winning!

Foreword

Unleashed and Unafraid

Unleashed and Unafraid is an extraordinary work that recounts Dr. Sabrena's personal journey. It is a genius galvanization of women who, through brilliant storytelling, counsel us to stretch beyond our perceived limitations to make a meaningful difference in the world.

This cleverly-written book is filled with inspirational stories of educators, writers, fashion designers, playwrights, technological innovators, attorneys, artists, and entrepreneurs who launched companies, engineered creative works, crafted brands, and built organizations that are shaping communities around the world.

Brimming with principles and life strategies, this book helps women take their place at decision-making tables and see themselves as part of the solution to the world's most pressing problems.

Dr. Sabrena and her sixteen accomplished colleagues are the personification of innovation, courage, and thought leadership. Their transformational stories will dispel the anxiety and misperceptions that have stopped most women from pursuing their dreams.

This book serves as a personal challenge to step away from the sidelines of life and lead with unflinching resolve. A page-turner, *Unleashed and Unafraid* is written to empower every reader to take their place amongst a disrupter-generation of women who are not bound to the status quo but are willing to embrace the distinctive role God has given them to lead change. This literary opus is a tour de force of seventeen courageous thinkers who share their heart in a refreshingly relatable way.

Dr. Sabrena Davis' book speaks to the genius within us all. *Unleashed and Unafraid* is a magnificent example of what we can do when we excavate our unique gifts and talents, while garnering the courage to build industry-specific platforms that allow our voices to be heard.

Dr. N. Cindy Trimm
Life Strategist, Author, Humanitarian

UNLEASHED AND UNAFRAID

TABLE OF CONTENTS

1	Pastor Martha Kure – Extraordinary Leadership	13
2	Ms. Jenell Ross – Owning Leadership	23
3	Ms. Charlotte Wilson – Beautiful Leadership	29
4	Ms. Janet Edmondson – Mediating Leadership	35
5	Mrs. Sherida McMullan – Tech Savvy Leadership	41
6	Dr. Donna Henry – Equilibrial Leadership	47
7	Ms. Debbie Chang – Legal Leadership	54
8	Ms. Laura Turner – Familial Leadership	62
9	Dr. Charrita Danely – Penning Leadership	68
10	Ms. Carolyn Mack – Persevering Leadership	75
11	Mrs. Veriner James – Heart Leadership	80
12	Ms. Sabrina Valdez – Prolific Leadership	86
13	Dr. Briancca Marshall – Pharmaceutical Leadership	93
14	Ms. Leia Avery – Disruptive Leadership	99
15	Mrs. Valdavia Ellis – Tailor Made Leadership	105
16	Lady Hendro Masenya – Leaderized Leadership	112

Introduction

Today, it is essential that women take the courage to lead intentionally. The strategic leadership of women results in the nurturing, rearing, and catapulting of generations. Featured unleashed and unafraid exemplars serve as living proof. Each leads through humility, positively influencing her own life and transforming the lives of others. All take calculated risks and walk by faith. Each understands the significance of reflecting on the past, optimizing the present and planning for the future. Each has garnered the strength to persevere and boldly walk in their greatness against all odds. Like you, some had to decide to move past painful pasts, give up toxic relationships, and abandon unfruitful friendships and mediocre lifestyle choices to excel in leadership and in life. Such decisions have ultimately blessed their lives, their families and their work.

My exemplars are not alone in demonstrating that generations are transformed through the excellent leadership of courageous women. Allow me to introduce five women whose intentional courageous action changed the law in a male-oriented society: the daughters of Zelophehad: Mahlah, Noah, Hoglah, Milcah, and Tirzah. Their story is found in the Bible in Numbers 27:1-7.

These five sisters came boldly to a tent meeting before Israel's leader Moses, Eleazar the priest, leaders, and the congregation contesting God's decree regarding the apportioning of "the promised land." God told Moses to allocate the land according to the number of names listed in each tribe that were counted in the census as recorded in Numbers 26:52-56. This decree posed a problem for the daughters of Zelophehad. Only men were counted in the census and were appropriated land at this time; therefore, his daughters would not receive their father's inheritance. These sisters refused to accept this fate.

So, at a time when it was uncustomary, the daughters of Zelophehad decided to take the reins of their destiny and lead. Intentionally strategizing, they humbly, but boldly, appeared before Moses, Eleazar and the community of leaders, persuasively arguing that their father's lineage should not be cut off just because he didn't have a son and that legally they should indeed inherit their father's portion of land.

Regarding their cause, Moses consults God then God renders the decision supporting their argument and instructs Moses to give the daughters their father's inheritance. Their faith, courageous action, and sound argument won the hearty approval of God and the acceptance of man. This was not only a win for the daughters of Zelophehad; it was also an established win for generations of daughters to come. Their determination of leadership touched God, changed a decree and transformed a nation.

The women featured in this book are much like the daughters of Zelophehad. They have boldly taken their place in society, fulfilling their purpose and destiny through courageous leadership. You too have a great purpose here on earth. You are reading this book because it is your time to rise and lead on a higher level. Your leadership journey begins with you. The triumphant accounts of featured women will encourage you to enhance your personal leadership in every area of your life and gracefully challenge you to lead unleashed and unafraid across generations in the area of your gifting.

*I will instruct you and teach you in the way you should go;
I will counsel you [who are willing to learn] with
My eye upon you.*
(Psalm 32:8)

Attribute One
Extraordinary Leadership
Pastor Martha Kure

A wise Apostle admonished that when encountering prominent people, one should seek their story, not their glory. The profoundness of this statement resonated deeply upon meeting Pastor Martha Kure. Evidence of an unusual fortification of strength and power exuded from her petite frame as she entered the Throneroom Trust Sanctuary. The atmosphere suddenly shifted, resulting in intensified worship. She wore the presence of God like a tailored cloak. Conference attendees quickly bowed their heads, displaying honor and respect. Unmistakably, the woman who births and nurtures "Sons of God" from the Motherland had arrived. Although her likeness was unbeknownst to me, I recognized her by way of the spirit.

Beholding her could not compare with hearing her penetrating words packaged in the most revelatory message for which my spirit has been privy. Her command of the audience stalled all recording and forced a welcoming gaze. Pastor Martha drew us all (Apostles, Prophets, Kings, Pastors, men, women, youth, the wealthy and the poor) to the well and together we drank its sweet waters.

She preached on "Taking Dominion" from the perspective

of being made in the likeness and image of God (Genesis 1:26-29). Her distinction between "likeness" and "image" and their separate yet interconnected meanings illuminated my understanding of the characteristics of God and why He created both male and female. She iterated that we could never know God in His full expression unless we understood the purpose of both His "likeness" and "image". She further explained that *"It is in His dimension that we find full expression in the male and female and use that understanding to take dominion over our lives and everything around us."*

Completely absorbed in her message, I sat still and silent and dared not even take notes. Discovering my spiritual tape recorder, I grasped John 14:26 (*But the Comforter, which is the Holy Ghost, whom the Father will send in my name, he shall teach you all things, and bring all things to your remembrance, whatsoever I have said unto you*) on a deeper level. While all the messages shared at my first conference on the continent of Africa were potent, Pastor Martha's was Extraordinary! Even young adult and teen attendees were set ablaze. The Mother of the Motherland showed up and thrust us forward from heaven's throne room.

Trans-generational leaders and attendees, hankering for more, nearly bum-rushed the media booth immediately following the benediction to secure a copy of Pastor Martha's teaching. Even her husband and leader, Apostle Emmanuel Kure, instructed the media team to produce his personal copy before leaving the sanctuary. What an honor! When a General of the Kingdom who leads Kings and speaks into the lives of Presidents and high-ranking spiritual and worldly leaders is wowed to the point of asking for a recorded sermon, you know God has shown up in you in a very extraordinary way. That day, I quietly uttered "Brava, Pastor Martha" and have been loudly voicing my "bravas" ever since.

Upon meeting Pastor Martha, I instantly understood why I had not completed and released the manuscript for Unleashed And Unafraid Volume II. Although I had come to know of her through stories told by her beloved son, Daniel Kure, a release absent her story and those included herein would have resulted in a premature, delicately seasoned work. In other words, it would have been an ordinary book yielding fluffy results. Today, women need to encounter ready works that have been marinated in heavy seasoning to yield extraordinary results. For this reason, I met Pastor Martha at the right time, in the right place, in the right season for right purposes.

Spending intimate one-on-one time with her while inhaling the sweet Florida air soothed my soul. A peace came over me that I so desperately needed. It was if I were being kissed by the sun while being touched by God's finger of love. Learning of all the miracles God performed in her life sky-rocketed my faith. Who would have thought that this sweet woman had to travel on foot for miles, hide in bushes (while pregnant), and take refuge in the homes of other Christians to escape the clutches of Muslim Fanatics to get an education?

That would not be the last time Pastor Martha and her husband encountered Muslim Fanatics in Northern Nigeria and other spiritual wickedness in high places to execute God's assignments. The prices she has paid to learn and lead to "raise" others register off the human Richter scale. Any woman blessed enough to be in her presence should soak up her wisdom and take heed of her profound revelations. They made me take an introspective look at my life and leadership, producing a thirst to be a more impactful leader.

When asked, Pastor Martha shared that her revelation comes from the place of seeking God and nothing else. She is not interested in religiosity, but in the person of God. Despite her accomplishments, she is constantly learning the pathway of the spirit and training her mind to look deeper into what God desires most while seeking to please Him. This is how He gives her revelation and understating obtainable in time and seasons. Extraordinarily, she takes a humble posture and lives what God sees.

I conclude that God sees an extraordinary, courageous woman who is intentional about fulfilling her purpose of impacting generations and who understands that leadership is not just about producing followers but producing leaders. Her annual Apostolic and Prophetic Gathering of Women and her annual Singles and Marriage Prophetic Conference serve as proof. The former empowers international women to boldly address nations, cities and governments in prophetic prayer. The Singles and Marriage Conference targets young couples and upcoming leaders who converge to dive deep into leadership topics such as vision, management, gift discovery, fulfillment, and Truth. Young couples and leaders are coached and strengthened as they take their place in society, rescuing their generation from villages, cities and bushes and producing quality leadership in the world.

Since 2011, over 600 villagers have been successfully trained under her leadership. Six hundred resounds as a considerable number given there is no government financial support system, and participants travel for miles from their villages on foot. (I have walked along one of the unpaved roads and just getting to the camp is work in and of itself). The center is financed through the Kures, Throneroom Trust Ministries and support of ministry friends.

Positioned from a young girl to make a strong impact on others, Pastor Martha is leading generations to greatness in Nigeria and beyond through her strategic work in ministry and education. The co-founder and overseer of The Craft and Resource

Center on the campgrounds of Throneroom Trust Ministries in Kafanchan, Nigeria, Pastor Martha's leadership paves the way for holistic living, allowing adult students to transcend socioeconomic barriers. While many community leaders institute funded programs to aid undereducated adults, youth and vulnerable citizens, Pastor Martha empowers and equips them with the knowledge and entrepreneurial skills necessary to support their families and impact the advancement of villages and towns.

Curious as to why a family with the means to live comfortably anywhere in Nigeria would live and work in developing conditions, I eagerly inquired of Pastor Martha. She shared that the center was born out of a cry in her husband's life to fulfill God's purpose of reaching out to those without help and a voice. Her husband heard God say, "Stay in Kafachan"; she stands with him. They obeyed and their strategic leadership via the Craft and Resource Center is bearing much fruit. Through training classes at the Craft and Resource Center, Pastor Martha is leading students across generations, bringing them out of the shadows into the forefront as entrepreneurs with sustainable skills useful anywhere in the world: catering; braiding; sewing/knitting/; beading and jewelry crafting; and making sandals. Student products are made with quality and precision.

I would know, for I had my hair braided in the salon in addition to buying hand-made jewelry, enjoying food cooked in the café, and getting fitted for original, authentic Nigerian dresses. Pastor Martha presented me with picturesque apparel as a thank you for caring for her son (while he studied in America) and she gifted me with sandals made by students to wear and share with others in America. I looked and felt better than ever wearing my new Nigerian dresses, jewelry and sandals, and sporting my eye-catching braids. Knowing that my gifts and purchases directly supported Pastor Martha's vision of advancing the local economy enhanced my overall experience greatly. Prior to each class at the

Craft and Resource Center, students are taught spiritual skills to instill hope, discipline, responsibility, and perseverance. Pastor Martha stresses that "the unlocking of eternal sources is in the hand of Christ. Christ is the source of life." Once students have honed their holistic skills, Pastor Martha and her team provides them the opportunity to sell their products in a designated area of the campground known as the marketplace. Start-up boxes are given to graduates upon successful completion of the program to give them a practical start in life and restore their human dignity. Indeed, many graduates have gone on to complete formal education and are using their knowledge and skills to win souls and instill hope, operate businesses, and contribute to the economic structure of their villages.

Examples of success include young male graduates making shoes and selling them to sponsor their own education and women using their start-up sewing kits to make uniform sweaters for local schools. Pastor Martha's graduates confidently compete for contracts and continue to secure them. But they don't stop there. They teach and help others as Pastor Martha encourages the train the trainer model. Like most entrepreneurs, graduates experience challenges, but they persevere. Pastor Martha teaches them that "Whatever is born of God will not fail!"

Understanding that the greatest wealth on earth is human beings, Pastor Martha invests in generations. From the place of prayer, she deeply reflects and ponders, "What will happen in the next five generations?" The mere question leads leaders to shift our thinking from building futures to building and sustaining futures. For this purpose, Pastor Martha established the Water Brooks Pathway School for children. At Water Brooks Pathway, children are deliberately taught to be seekers and keepers of truth; to be people of influence in the world; to love and respect everyone regardless of religion, and to honor God and His word with quality education.

Core values such as Respect, hope, resilience, responsibility, and excellence underpin the curriculum. Children learn to literally drink from the water brook thereby rejecting lies, fear and lethargy. They graduate prepared to think critically and creatively, pursue higher education, speak truth with boldness, inspire their parents to excel, and work resiliently across the spectrum. High expectations and fortification rule at Waterbrook thanks to Pastor Martha's leadership.

A model leader, Pastor Martha is leading her staff in raising children and families that will bring influence in the villages, towns and country of Nigeria through education. While many school proprietors target the poor and ill-educated when establishing new schools, Pastor Martha targets the middle class. Evaluation of economic, political and social structures and trends has resulted in Pastor Martha's resolution that focusing on the success of the next generation alone will not produce the sustained outcomes we seek. We must go deeper by structuring school, ministry and work experiences in ways that will stimulate and strengthen families who will continue the cycle of positively affecting future generations.

Pastor Martha's strategy works. She and the Throneroom through the work of the Holy Spirit has influenced serious-minded, transforming middle-class citizens to return to and/or stay in Kafanchan to serve as signs of hope and work to grow the local economy. They have bought into Pastor Martha's vision and trust her and her team with the education of their children. Kafanchan now has quality schools, full functioning banks, restaurants, and civil service branches. Yes, even the government seeks to find its place in Pastor Martha's vision of entrepreneurship. They too see the incredible value in her trans-generational model and assuredly will use it to transform other villagers. "Brava, Pastor Martha."

As an author, educator, and watch woman who seeks to be more intimate with God, I admire Pastor Martha Kure. It is an honor to know her. She is transforming generations in ways that many only dream of. She is a daughter of God who operates in the earthly realm from heavenly places even in her work. This represents my striving in life. At a time when I needed it most, I read Pastor Martha's life-changing book *"Horizons of Sons."*

It is by far one of the best books for which I have ever engaged as it taught me who I am in God and bolstered strength and courage from a place inside of me that I had not discovered. After reflecting on the book three times, scriptures walked off the pages and led me down the pathway to God's water brook. Spiritual water never tasted so sweet. Astounding! Any time a leader's writing can pull you out of yourself although you are not in the same space, that's Extraordinary Leadership!

Both Pastor Martha and I come from humble beginnings, facing tumultuous challenges on our leadership journeys. The constant has always been our relationship with God and our obedience to His will for our lives. Impeccable results of our obedience are seen in our transformational work in leadership, ministry, schools and communities. Two of the most impressive works attributed to Pastor Martha and her husband Apostle Emmanuel Kure are the personal sponsorship of education for hundreds of youth and the building of the largest Prayer Tower in Northern Nigeria (in Kafanchan). Both speak volumes of their excellence in servant leadership and apostolic leadership.

Now, more than ever, humanity needs to take a lesson from all of creation and do as the scripture says, *"Watch and pray…"* (Matthew 26:41a). Each may be given a different burden for which to pray, but it is clear that prayer is essential for every area of our lives. And as Pastor Martha shared with me, *"Just as all the women in the bible were not doing the same thing, you need to ask*

God what He wants you to pray for and what He has for you. Even in leadership, don't be hasty to take action. Quietness is your confidence; it is the place of prayer and wisdom. Leadership born of the spirit will thrive. Get to the place where you rely on the Holy Spirit and teach others to do the same." This is the pinnacle of trans-generational, Extraordinary Leadership.

To what extent is your leadership impacting generations and pointing them to God? In what ways is it extraordinary? Is it extraordinarily temporary or eternal?

But remember the Lord your God, for it is he who gives you the ability to produce wealth, and so confirms his covenant, which he swore to your ancestors, as it is today.

(Deuteronomy 8:18)

Attribute Two
Owning Leadership
Ms. Jenell Ross

In the world where St. John, Intel, Coca-Cola and others intersected, there stood a humble woman whose silhouette gleamed from afar. Almost unnoticed, one may have easily missed her amidst the crowd of dancing women. Somehow, our eyes connected.

Meeting Ms. Jenell Ross was one of the highlights of my journey into the world of Odyssey Media, a minority female-owned company that connects and cultivates like-minded affluent and influential multicultural women from across the globe. To say that the Odyssey Conference is something from another planet would be an understatement. Imagine a dimension where over 600 of the most powerful, influential women in the world gather for a week for empowering, exploring, networking, spending and having incalculable fun. Now further imagine a dimension where your nightly entertainment and empowerment sessions are facilitated by world-class performers and experts. Prevailing in this dimension can only mean one thing for its resident women: they Own Leadership. This concept fits Jenell Ross like St. John apparel fits supermodel Garcelle Beauvais.

Ms. Ross must have known that I was new to the Odyssey experience as she introduced herself followed by a welcoming handshake. Who was I that she would introduce herself, a long-time member of the Odyssey Network? Who was she that I would find myself in her graces? Our intriguing conversation would soon reveal all.

As we conversed, Ms. Ross inquired about my road to Odyssey. I shared that I am an educator who was invited by my Chief Academic Officer as a reward for my hard work. She smiled and asked what else I aspired to do in life. Intriguing! Usually, people ask educators about our opinions regarding educational policy, the validity of standardized tests, and educational equity. Thankfully, I had just approved the cover of Unleashed And Unafraid Volume I earlier that day. That allowed me to boldly declare that I aspire to be an affluent, world-known author. The opportunity presented itself to tell someone other than my team members that I was a new author, so I took it. Ms. Ross displayed excitement then probed deeper, asking about the legacy of my family. I shared that my family's gifts are rooted in the arts and that my husband aspires to own an auto dealership. Bingo! We reached the tipping point.

Ms. Ross' face brightened at the mention of my husband's owning an automobile dealership. Had I come all the way to Naples, Florida to meet a woman who would be instrumental in my husband's entrepreneurial venture and our family's legacy? Without hesitation, Ms. Ross asked an array ofo questions about my husband's journey in the auto industry. The conclusion of our highly engaging conversation, Ms. Ross gave me her business card and asked me to share her contact information with my husband.

The next night, she introduced me to an African-American gentleman who owns a dealership in Naples, Florida and welcomed my husband to connect with him as well. She knew what I did not know and I am happy that thoughts of insecurity didn't ruin my opportunity to connect her and my husband and even more, my opportunity to share her illustration of Owning Leadership with the world.

Just who is Ms. Jenell Ross? I couldn't get to my fancy room fast enough to google her. My eyes widened as I read her profile and her family's history. On my first night at Odyssey, I made acquaintance with "The" Jenell Ross, CEO of the Bob Ross Auto Group in Centerville, Ohio. If any woman knows about owning leadership through the spirit of humility, it's Jenell Ross.

Articles featuring Ms. Ross and her extraordinary story are housed on various internet sites. Herein are highlights that epitomize her as one who is unleashed and unafraid to own leadership. In a male-dominated industry, Ms. Ross became President of the Bob Ross Auto Group at age 27 after the death of her father. Since that time, she has been leading the charge. Included in her company's portfolio are Buick-GMC-Mercedes-Benz, Alfa Romeo and Fiat dealerships.

Clearly, she owns her world. Spending time working in the dealership throughout high school and college coupled knowledge and skills learned from her studies at Emory University (Atlanta), the General Motors Dealer Management Development Program and the National Automobile Dealers Association Dealer Candidate Academy no doubt prepared her for her role as CEO & President. What a great attributing to her parents, the late Mr. Robert and Mrs. Norma J. Ross, who were the first African-American Mercedes-Benz dealers in the world.

Learning this valuable piece of information from Ms. Ross helped me to understand why she asked about my family's legacy and my personal aspirations. She was not merely asking; she was emphasizing their pertinence. Ms. Ross demonstrates that women who own leadership lead others to their greatness.

Today, Ms. Jenell Ross is not only recognized as a distinguished leader in the auto industry, she is a driving force in raising breast cancer awareness and inspiring youth. In honor of her mother, she established the "The Norma J. Ross Youth Foundation" and "Pink Ribbon Driven Campaign" to benefit youth and to raise money for breast cancer research. What an excellent way to honor one's parent and sustain the family legacy. Notably, great leaders lead across generations by honoring the past, cultivating the present and birthing the future. Such is the impressive case of Ms. Jenell Ross. Because she owns leadership, Ms. Ross' skill set transcends the skills required for specific industries. Her leadership runs the gamut and generations are being catapulted as a result.

Moreover, under Ms. Ross' leadership, the Ross Auto Group serves as a major sponsor of the "Making Strides Against Breast Cancer Walk." Through this medium, Ms. Ross and her team raise awareness and funds that support the American Cancer Society. Monies are used for breast cancer screening and early detection; aiding in the reduction of breast cancer risks; funding innovative breast cancer research; providing free information; and supporting programs to patients and caregivers. Her team even outfits the dealerships in pink during October to share solidarity.

Additionally, Ms. Ross serves as a national advocate for diversity and minority entrepreneurs. She is the only second-generation African American female-franchised automobile dealership owner in the U.S. and was the first African American woman elected to chair the American International Automobile Dealers Association (AIADA).

Are you ready for the icing on the cake? With all of her accomplishments and accolades, Ms. Ross walks in humility. That is the very thing that attracted me to her. A multidimensional leader in education and the leader of the Unleashed And Unafraid Movement, I know my craft well and am leading others to greatness through humility.

As an entrepreneur, I diligently seek opportunities to hone my craft by learning from model leaders like Ms. Ross, for she intentionally Owns Leadership in ways that make others take note. I surely did.

What steps are you taking to own leadership?

I praise you because I am fearfully and wonderfully made;
your works are wonderful,
I know that full well.
(Psalm 139:14)

Attribute Three
Beautiful Leadership
Ms. Charlotte Wilson

Beautiful leadership requires honing one's awareness, building relationships and taping into the emotions of others. Women who are unleashed and unafraid to lead their lives are intentionally aware of who they are, where they are in life and where they are going. Such awareness drives their strategic decisions on building relationships and tapping into the emotional self-interest of others.

It has been stated that beauty is pleasurable; it has also been iterated that beauty goes deeper than the surface. Both are true and relevant to my leadership exemplar, CEO Charlotte Wilson. Further, most if not all leadership gurus would argue that a powerful synonym for leadership is "influence." When you combine holistic elements of beauty and leadership, what is produced is an alluring essence of influence that is deeply satisfying to the mind, eye, and soul.

The CEO and Founder of Glow Skin Enhancement, Ms. Charlotte Wilson exemplifies beauty in every sense of the word. One gaze upon her flawless bronzed skin provokes an inward sense of betterment. Women with her level of outward beauty always look like they are walking in slow motion forcing others to take notice. Equally important, one conversation with her urges women to take the next step of enhancing their own beauty. And at this, she is the master. After all, she is the face of the company. From our first encounter at a Women's Expo in Atlanta, it was clear that Ms. Charlotte understood that when you look good, you feel good. This may sound cliché, but not all women grasp the power or simplicity of this concept.

Ms. Charlotte and I exchanged glances a few times at the busy expo, but audience engagement delayed our meeting until the last day. She took the lead. Trusting her leadership qualities, Ms. Charlotte presented a gift accompanied by a genial introduction. Her approach appealed to both my business and emotional consciousness. Just like that, she negotiated a trade: Glow Skin Enhancement products for an autographed copy of Unleashed And Unafraid. The most beautiful part is that she bartered without a conversation. Perhaps she observed the make-up artist pampering my face just before my seminar delivery. Perhaps she noticed skin imperfections and targeted me as a future client. Perhaps something arose compelling her to make acquaintance at an opportune time. Whatever the reason, Ms. Charlotte demonstrated how to network, lead an impactful dialogue and deliver the best one-minute elevator speech while leaving an indelible impression. Instead of pointing out flaws and attempting to sell products to address them, Ms. Charlotte simply gifted me with products and asked for honest feedback in return. This is Beautiful Leadership at its best.

Indulging in my new Glow Skin Enhancement products reigned upon my return home. As the company claims, my skin was renewed, restored and enhanced. No stranger to acne, dullness and discoloration, my face was grateful for new friends. Not a day or evening was skipped in using the face cleansers and moisturizers. The results were amazing: clear, soft skin with a glow. After a few days of use, many complimented the improvements while some whispered speculations of pregnancy.

Flattering! Ms. Charlotte transformed my thinking around beauty. Learning more about her became inevitable.

Ms. Charlotte Wilson ranks among America's top beauty moguls. She is not only beautiful but brilliant and resilient. Gracing the cover of magazines and headlining at expos and events, Ms. Charlotte owns her world. As Founder and CEO of Glow Skin Enhancement, she honed the entrepreneurial skills necessary to build and sustain an empire. Ms. Charlotte, like many entrepreneurs, birthed and sustains her business through diligence and tenacity. She uses research and a human-centered approach of trial and error to bring her visions to life. Her Glow Skin Enhancement line offers unique solutions for everyone and all skin types. With a great understanding of the ideation process combined with the needs of end users, she consistently produces quality skincare products used by celebrities and everyday people alike. In fact, Ms. Charlotte proclaims that Glow Skin Enhancement is more than just a luxury skin line; it is an empowerment luxury skin care company. Proof speaks.

The consistency and quality of products has led to the establishment of her GSE Beauty Ambassadors City Program. Brand Ambassadors enjoy the benefits of the program including product use, client connections, and an entrepreneurial opportunity with a flourishing company. One can find Glow Skin Enhancement products in Atlanta and surrounding cities in Georgia; Beverly Hills and Hollywood, California; and Houston, Texas. Products will be available soon in Chicago, Illinois; Miami and Palm Beach, Florida; and a city near you. Ms. Charlotte is truly a super entrepreneur who is deliberately paving the way for others.

All great leaders add value to those they serve and leave a legacy for those they love. Ms. Charlotte Wilson models both. She built her personal brand and her company through networking and nurturing meaningful relationships with local communities and businesses. This is how we made our acquaintance. People see her as an asset to the community and therefore trust her guidance. Moreover, as a mother of five, Ms. Charlotte lives for the present and future. She is providing a good life for her children while intentionally building a legacy of love, service, and wealth. That's Beautiful Leadership!

Reflecting on Ms. Charlotte's incredible journey brings to mind my intentionality around beautifully leading generations. A scripture that highly resonates is Romans 10:15 (NIV), *"And how can anyone preach unless they are sent? As it is written: 'How beautiful are the feet of those who bring good news!'"* One of my purposes is to teach and galvanize generations of women to own their personal power and have an impact on others. This is accomplished through Unleashed And Unafraid seminars, webinar courses, book talks and coaching. The transformation of lives through my heartfelt work produces inner and outer beauty. Admittedly, leadership, transformation and empowerment are exquisitely attractive. Similar to Ms. Charlotte's, my clients often comment that they not only feel better about themselves after our encounters, but they feel empowered to take the courage to lead their own lives. Beautiful!

One well-known contemporary Christian artist, Danny Gokey, sings a song that partially encapsulates lessons learned about Beautiful Leadership from Ms. Charlotte Wilson's life: *The Comeback*. The song opens with powerful lyrics that remind all to own your life. The bridge of the song further encourages and strengthens, resonating with the beautiful leader inside us all. The overarching message is *Keep Going*! Despite the challenges, setbacks, and heartbreaks, take the reins and govern your beautiful life. Decide today to let your "inner queen" arise and take her place on the throne of society. Adorn your "outer queen" with humility, strength, and luxurious Glow Skin Enhancement products.

As the famous adage suggests, "When you look good, you feel better." Ms. Charlotte came to this realization a long time ago and decided to lead the charge in helping others become their best beautiful selves. Correspondingly, my understanding of the correlation between beauty and leadership enhanced my productivity along with my levels of confidence and influence. Good news: Anyone can claim the understanding and realization of beautiful leadership. Beautiful Leadership is not reserved for the rich and famous. With diligence and tenacity mixed with strategic intentionality, it is yours for the taking. With one life to live, lead it beautifully. It's your time: Rise up; come back; Lead Beautifully!

Stop judging by mere appearances, but instead judge correctly.
(John 7:24)

Attribute Four
Mediating Leadership
Ms. Janet Edmondson

Lights, center-stage, shoes, action! Walk this way if you dare. Be careful, for the shoes you slip your feet into to walk someone else's path might not only hurt, but squeeze the judgment right out of you. In fact, her signature plays, *Walk In My Shoes I & II* are produced to do just that. Sold-out, spell-bound audiences walk away reformed with a clearer understanding of grace. Just who is this courageous writer, producer and director shaking up major cities with the ageless idiom *Walk In My Shoes*? She is Ms. Janet Edmondson.

Through her signature plays, *Walk In My Shoes I & II*, Ms. Janet revolutionizes the way people look at others; encourages women to suspend judgment while offering support towards other women; and strongly contends that despite calamitous circumstances, resilient women always land on their feet with the grace to keep walking. The content of *Walk In My Shoes I & II* influences the mindset of critics and well-wishers. Critics ruminate on their insulting behavior seeking strategies of change while well-wishers direct their energy in more strategic ways to encourage others. Both groups find themselves identifying with the experience(s) of one or more of the characters and exercising what leadership guru John C. Maxwell refers to as *The Law of Reflection* (from the book *The 15 Invaluable Laws of Growth*). Maxwell teaches that everyone should learn to pause intentionally to reflect then turn those reflections into practical insights. Ms. Janet has mastered this process and serves as the ultimate mediator through the creative genius of *Walk In My Shoes I & II* and *Big Shoes To Feel: Men's Edition*.

My first viewing of *Walk In My Shoes I* was nearly accidental. Plans called for travel with a last minute decision to cancel to support cast members who happened to be mentees and a long-time friend. The pounding in my heart could be heard across the room as I waited for the Eventbrite page to load. After all, there was much buzz around this production. The fact that it was being performed at the historic DuSable Museum in Chicago added to the intensity. When the page finally loaded, the phrase "2 remaining" jumped off the page so I jumped at the opportunity to load my credit card information to purchase one of them. With 40 minutes to show time, I made a mad dash, eager to get a good seat. Whew, I made it!

An actress myself, I appreciated the passion and energy of each actor in bringing the 12 characters to life in very memorable ways. Their lines still speak. Audience members unashamedly expressed a range of diverse emotions as they journeyed with each character. Whether it was the cancer victor, battered wife, police officer, bride-to-be, gambler, recovering addict or others, the thickness of empathy could be felt throughout the auditorium. Experiencers even remained seated during intermission to absorb every moment.

At the conclusion of the curtain call, I rushed to stand in line to congratulate Ms. Janet. She was a bit overwhelmed with all the praise and exhilaration, so my comment was succinct. We embraced and I said, *"Everyone needs to see this play. When I went online to buy my ticket, there were only two left. Glad I got mine. God bless you. I am going to spread the word and can't wait to see the next show."* She smiled and said, *"Oh, thank you very much!"* Two days later, while speaking with Principal Donna Henry, one of the characters I happened to coach at the time, she shared that Ms. Janet received words from a young lady after the production that really encouraged her and she wished she knew the young lady. Principal Henry asked if I spoke those words to her aunt, Ms. Janet. I smiled and politely affirmed with a head nod. *Small world!* With this new connection, I wasted no time in asking for a formal introduction.

Our enchanting dialogue resulted in the blossoming of a beautiful, collaborative relationship. Ms. Janet, along with actresses Donna Henry and Yvonne Griffin, graced my *Unleashed And Unafraid Broadcast*, adding value to my viewing audience (**https://youtu.be/xN1EgoSmc3o**). In the interview, Ms. Janet discussed overcoming trials and tribulations by the grace of God, the inspiration behind writing *Walk In My Shoes*, and the need to suspend judgment and understand what others go through just to live. Both actresses portrayed a snippet of their unforgettable characters… just enough to whet appetites, enticing prospective audiences. I contributed to her work by using my platform to attract new audiences. It worked. Great things happen when leaders intentionally mediate processes.

The "Why" behind Ms. Janet's urgency to finally produce and bring *Walk In My Shoes* to the masses bears emotion that propels mediation. Her granddaughter, Nya Lamarre, passed away four years after being diagnosed with a malignant brain tumor. Aware of Ms. Janet's manuscript, Nya had hopes of playing a role in *Walk In My Shoes*. Sadly, Princess Nya did not get an opportunity to play a role as Ms. Janet had not yet completed the manuscript. Honorably, the first production of *Walk In My Shoes* was presented on Nya's birthday. Although Ms. Janet does not play a character, her decision to present the play on her beloved granddaughter's birthday in and of itself is a play on the idiom *"Walk in my shoes."* Two lessons she clearly mediated are do not judge others as you haven't a clue what they have endured nor what it took for them to triumph and make the decision to intentionally move within the grace of God so that you do not have to walk in some shoes.

Ms. Janet has found a way to artistically intervene in the lives of others, greatly influencing changes in behavior. Her call to action through *Walk In My Shoes* compels others to join her in mediating on behalf of all who need encouragement, exhortation, and admonition. She has been divinely appointed to mediate intra- and interpersonal dualities. Her mediating leadership has positively impacted the mindsets of community leaders, forging the necessary balance of pressure and support. Ms. Janet has demonstrated that the notion of *Mediating Leadership* must be intentionally modeled and implemented by courageous women to produce systematic change and yield personal growth. Ms. Janet offers a blueprint. To what extent are we bold enough to follow it?

Mediating Leadership requires objectivity, empathy and the ability to facilitate life-changing moments and experiences. It also requires a great level of humility. Using these attributes as metrics, Ms. Janet and I excel in this process. Like Ms. Janet, I design human-centered, transformative experiences that help people reflect, grow and change. Such experiences take on the form of webinars; face-to-face training and coaching; interactive book dialogues; and my signature *Unleashed And Unafraid* Women's Galvanization Conference and Seminars. Clients and participants never leave the same way they arrived, for I have learned the art diagnosing the condition of mindsets followed by skillful mediating of current and potential dualities. I boldly articulate my motives to extinguish suspicion and intellectual fear. Make no mistake; there is no room for manipulation when respectfully mediating and leading others. This represents a premise of the *Unleashed And Unafraid Movement*.

The release of *Unleashed And Unafraid* and *Walk In My Shoes* comes at a great time in history. Both movements are led by humble, yet, courageous leaders destined to transform our worlds and impact others to transform theirs. We invite you to join us in the process of *Mediating Leadership* in your family, community, and places where you work and play. Your world is waiting on you and the leadership only you can provide. Someone needs you to intercede on her/his behalf.

Someone needs you to model the ways of success. Still, others need you to teach, guide, and counsel in order that they may make sound decisions that will perhaps save their lives. From this moment forward, resolve to lead. Implement the solutions that are sizzling in your bones. See yourself as Mediating Leadership and then do it. This is one of the few times in life where I encourage you to *Walk In Our Shoes*!

*A man's heart deviseth his way:
but the LORD directeth his steps.
(Proverbs 16:9)*

Attribute 5
Tech-Savvy Leadership
Mrs. Sherida McMullan

"That's what technology looks like," declared the animated announcer. Whatever perception of technology inhabited the forefront of my mind before observing her strut down the runway in shimmering tech gear instantly changed after she sat and unveiled her costume mask. Never before had technology carried an ambrosial smell or bequeathed a rousing sight. Every woman in the room marveled, rose hastily, and clapped thunderously after the sexy tech fashion show. While each tech model rocked, my gaze was fixed on Mrs. Sherida McMullan.

On the afternoon following the sexy tech fashion show, Sherida and I ended up in concurring workshops. The chances of this occurring with over 20 simultaneous workshops were unlikely. Imagine the joy leaping in my belly. Normally, I sit at the front of the room to minimize distractions. On this occasion, I intentionally claimed a seat at a table behind Sherida's. She stood out amid the other women and my hunger to know her had to be satisfied.

Midway through the workshop, the facilitator provided a response to a participant's question to which Sherida disagreed. With confidence and humility, she challenged the facilitator's response and line of thinking so authoritatively that the facilitator had to pause and reflect. Sherida used the design thinking approach to affect the mindset of participants.

It is still unclear if others recognized her strategy. A fan of design thinking, I discerned her approach immediately. She brilliantly put a tech spin on a common issue and walked us through a creative process to solve it using tech terminology. Every woman in the room was a boss, but Sherida was clearly the leader.

Events of the second session bear a permanent brand. Another well-known facilitator, more in-depth questions posed by intelligent, affluent women and another star-studded performance by Sherida. This time, I was the object of her "sheroism." The facilitator presented information and demonstrations around highly sensitive issues. At moments, I was baffled…at other times, embarrassed and hurt. Judging from my colleagues engaging interactions, they had it all together and I was just scratching the surface. Sure, I held a high position (Superintendent) in my company, but I held a low perspective in a particular area. The worst part is that I was not aware prior to this workshop. This proves that there is always a need for growth and development. One may master one area, but she may be a novice in another.

Sherida quickly noticed the change in my complexion and disposition. A true leader, she ministered to me in the session despite a captive audience. Her authenticity broke the dam and my well of tears flowed. After the room cleared, she asked two questions that got at the heart of the matter and listened attentively as I responded. She did not just hear me, she listened. This allowed her to further console me and outline a growth plan specific to my dilemma.

Did all tech-savvy women operate in this fashion? Were they trained to see the world through a tech lens? I wondered. Could technology really solve a personal problem that greatly affected my heart? What greater lesson was I to learn from this experience perfectly designed by God?

While the answer to these questions did not immediately surface, Sherida had solved a very personal problem that haunted me and stunted my growth using tech tools. Impressive! Her experiences in the tech world were needed to impact my life at the right time. Whatever fear and intimidation of technology I had prior to our encounter dissipated that day. Similar to the announcer of the fashion show, I found myself iterating, *"Now that's what technology looks like! Sherida McMullan is what tech-savvy leadership looks like."* And wow was she awesome.

One has to know her unique background to fully appreciate Sherida's leadership destiny. Since her preschool days, Sherida has always been interested in technology and math. She is employed by one of the largest tech companies in the world. As a matter of fact, the company holds a high rank on the Fortune 500 list for computer software and information companies known for designing and manufacturing digital technology products. It takes a skilled, confident and savvy woman who is totally unleashed and unafraid to produce in such a company. This is especially true for African-American women who traditionally make-up the most under-represented group in the field. Bracingly, the company provides a sophisticated echelon of diversity practices aimed at hiring, retaining and fully representing tech-savvy women and underrepresented minorities. Sherida represents both categories, making the two a perfect match.

From a young age, Sherida has had a fascination with technology underpinned by a love for math. In third grade, Sherida's teacher, Mrs. Robinson, quickly recognized her love for math and encouraged her to cultivate it. Supportively, Mrs.

Robinson differentiated her instruction, providing opportunities for young Sherida to move into advanced problem solving. The only African-American in the class, Sherida stood out and her "hidden figures" journey began to emerge. It did not take her long to see the strong correlation between math and technology.

All roads led to the pursuit of an Electrical Engineering degree at the prestigious Howard University, a Historically Black College & University. The atmosphere at Howard offered Sherida an opportunity to learn and lead. An El Paso, Texas native who grew up in a multicultural environment, she thought she needed the black experience to round out her life.

In her own words, "*Little did I know that growing up in El Paso shaped me as a bilingual woman and allowed me to thrive in any environment. It also was instrumental in how I raised my daughter. She is fully bilingual and reads, writes, and speaks Spanish fluently.*" Her story is repeating itself. That's good leadership.

While pursuing her degree at Howard University, Sherida did several internships and co-ops. She chose not to pursue employment with interning companies because they were focused on isolated fields that did not include interactions with people. Smart woman! It was clear to everyone around her that she not only had a love for technology and math, but she had a love for leadership. In her senior year, she learned of the Technical Sales Engineer role at a top technology company from a recruiter at the job fair who happened to be former classmate. In that position, she would be on the cutting edge of technology, able to utilize her technology expertise by breaking down the concepts into everyday terms to educate limited tech users.

Sherida resolved that she had found her calling. Like all great leaders, she had a laser focus on finding a company that met her criteria: cutting-edge technology, growth company, excellent salary, and warm weather. Like all great leaders, she knew that if she were thriving in her position, she could lead and serve others better.

Both Sherida and I are unleashed and unafraid to lead through servant leadership. We thrive on opportunities to collaborate with others who think differently and create solutions to complex problems. Although this is rarely an easy process, it teaches us to open our minds and allow for other leaders, ideas, and processes to stimulate our growth and enrich our influence. This is exactly what occurred the day I met Ms. Sherida. The servant leader in her recognized the complexity of my problem and stepped up to encourage and support me from a fresh perspective using her tech expertise. I grew tremendously and my personal leadership has been forever enhanced through her leadership. Because of that very interaction with Sherida, I have a newfound respect for tech tools and the women who use them adeptly. My hope is that more girls and women will pursue degrees and careers in the tech industry like Sherida McMullan.

Leadership, education, and sponsorship are key. Together, these three will equip female champions and male allies with the right tools to sponsor the future generations of female tech enthusiasts. The value-add of female leadership in technology is often overlooked. Thanks to the Tech-Savvy Leader, Sherida McMullan, we have all been enlightened. Let us all turn a new page and get our tech on. Let us serve the next generations well by leading them to use technology properly to improve their lives and generate societal solutions. It's sexy to be tech-savvy. One view of Sherida McMullan will make you a believer. And that, my friends, is what technology looks like!

And we know that in all things God works for the good of those who love him, who have been called according to his purpose.
(Romans 8:28)

Attribute 6
Equilibrial Leadership
Dr. Donna Henry

Dr. Donna Henry is an educational "Super Star." She lives and leads a balanced life intentionally. Dr. Henry spends as much time developing her personal life (taking real vacations, supporting her nephews at athletic competitions, serving in her church, and acting) as she does her work life (leading schools, facilitating professional development, supervising and evaluating teachers, and nurturing students). For the past six years, I have watched her bloom into an Equilibrial Leader.

Achieving equilibria requires precision and strategy. Dr. Henry possesses both. She is equally good at providing instructional leadership as she is managing people, budgets, and operations. As defined on dictionary.com, _equilibria is a condition in which all influences acting upon it are canceled by others, resulting in a stable, balanced, or unchanging system._ Webster defines _equilibria_ as _a state of intellectual or emotional balance._ These definitions suggest that some people and/or systems actually gain stability and balance in the middle of struggle and torque. This way of thinking may seem counterintuitive, but it is quite fascinating. So is watching Dr. Henry navigate through processes and manage influencers and influences.

I remember when Dr. Henry was a young, ambitious Assistant Principal. Her ability to problem-solve under pressure quickly gained the respect of the entire school community. No task was too menial and no request too big. With a spirit of humility, she consistently went above and beyond the call of duty. After working with her as one of her Supervising Directors, she approached me with a dilemma. The potential consequences could have put our new school project at risk.

She reminded me of a statement I made in my introduction to the school's leadership team: *"Please think through solutions before presenting problems."* Afterwards, she presented the troubling dilemma with well-thought-out solutions. Dr. Henry's ability to balance emotions and reasoning in the midst of confusion wrought by diverse authoritative influences was impressive. Her bold move brought calmness and stability to a new team.

Intrigued by this young, wise administrator, I began to observe her closely. Dr. Henry was the "real deal." What stood out most was her balanced skill set. She was a skilled and competent instructional leader as well as a skilled, efficient manager of people and processes. Being equally adept at both as a fairly new administrator is rare. Other leaders and influencers also took note. Like a mother eagle, I personally took a vested interest in her leadership development and became very protective. I understood the trials, triumphs and hard lessons learned in being a young school administrator in threatening environments with intentionally problematic stakeholders. I overcame and my goal was to ensure Dr. Henry did the same. Soon, we had a developed a trustful relationship that today I deeply cherish.

In less than a year, the young Donna Henry was unanimously voted in as Principal of a historic high school in Gary, Indiana - a state takeover school with more than 16 years of failure. It was the perfect clash between seen and unseen forces purposefully designed to demonstrate equilibria. God handpicked administrators and staff and, at the right time, appointed a leader whom He had groomed through her personal experiences. She was ready. Knowing the academic, cultural, and political challenges helped.

In many of our coaching sessions, I asked questions about Dr. Henry's personal life to get a greater sense of the inward place from which she led. What I came to realize is that she had been contending to sustain the balanced life that she had achieved through tumultuous times both in her pre and post-college years. She and I often discussed spiritual and natural implications of decision-making based on experience, research, observations and scripture. As she allowed, I even inquired of her decisions around her personal and spiritual relationships. My inquiries were sincerely addressed, further highlighting her sense of equilibria.

Dr. Henry's capacity to maintain balance in the storm was immediately and repeatedly tested. Shortly after she was appointed Principal, I was appointed Superintendent. Before we could celebrate, the war games began. Attacks from diverse stakeholders emerged from the land, sea and air. Everything that could go wrong with a school building went wrong: bursting pipes, flooding, frigid temperatures, loss of air conditioning in summers, loss of heat in winters, lack of water, etc.

One year, we had to close school for eight consecutive days due to lack of heat. Local and state-wide stakeholders expressed their anger and even disrupted the learning environment by showing up with media unannounced, spewing untruths and harshly questioning us in the presence of staff and students. We endured these attacks and conditions for five years. It was disheartening at times, but we knew that we had the fortitude to stabilize outside forces for the sake of the students and staff we served.

Remarkably, Dr. Henry managed to focus on successfully implementing her school improvement plan, raising student achievement, growing her teachers and staff, and developing her administrators all while in the "eye of the storm". Many young Principals, especially those who like Dr. Henry are very strong instructional leaders, would have walked away and landed a Principalship at a school with less political turmoil and way better working conditions. She stayed and she remained in control. Dr. Henry achieved equilibrial leadership, defying odds and closing mouths. BAM! She earned my respect and the title, "*Super Star.*"

Under her leadership, school climate shifted from disrespectful to respectful; school pride went from indifferent to enthusiastic; discipline infractions and suspensions decreased dramatically; test scores increased; teachers became leaders; and a sense of family was adopted in the hearts of students and staff. The Indiana State Board of Education publicly recognized the work of "Super Star" Principal Henry and her team in building and sustaining healthy school culture.

My chest puffed like a peacock's when the school received this prestigious recognition. The work of the leadership team led by Dr. Henry was intentional. Building a healthy school culture where students felt safe and cared for topped the list. She worked diligently with the leadership team and Achievement Directors to develop a philosophy of discipline to override the issuance of arbitrary detentions, suspensions and expulsions. Development of a school-wide philosophy of discipline resulted in a systematic approach and well-defined process that clearly aligned infractions with mandatory and optional consequences, addressed the roots of discipline issues, and supported multi-level learning. Fidelity of implementation allowed staff to focus on redirecting students and teaching appropriate behaviors as opposed to constantly suspending and expelling students.

Undoubtedly, some students committed infractions that warranted both and a few refused to adhere to this equitable practice. Nevertheless, Dr. Henry and her staff stuck to the process. While many school administrators rid themselves of "problem students" through the suspension and expulsion process, she led her team to partner with students to identify and correct unwanted behaviors. Students who would have otherwise been expelled learned how to manage and adjust. As a result, suspensions and expulsions decreased, classroom management improved, and the instruction progressed. What a perfect example of equilibrial leadership underpinned by wisdom. For all who may not be aware, the use of wisdom and compassion in dealing with students keeps everyone safe!

Of all the Principals I have coached, Dr. Henry's experience mirrors mine the most. Our humble beginnings in school leadership were filled with repugnant encounters designed to make us quit. I personally know many school leaders who have done just that in similar situations. No judgments here. Only God's grace coupled with the knowledge that education is a mountain we must rule has sustained us and catapulted us to success. Furthermore, our ability to balance leadership and life allows us to think clearly, make wise decisions, help others, and maintain the level of health needed to truly lead.

Dr. Henry's equilibrial leadership stretches across generations in multiple areas. She cognizes both the meaning and benefit of leading a balanced life and influences others through her actions. When not working, she can be found announcing at her church, supporting her nephews in their baseball and basketball games/tournaments, performing as a lead actress in the hit play *Walk In My Shoes*, and riding her pink Harley Davidson (prophetically speaking).

This helps others understand that it is much easier to *lead* when you know how to bring balance to your own life. It works for Dr. Henry and it works for me. It will work for you too.

How are you working toward Equilibrial Leadership?

So in everything, do to others what you would have them do to you, for this sums up the Law and the Prophets.
(Matthew 7:12)

Attribute Seven
Legal Leadership
Ms. Deborah Chang

Never wish away a cold winter day, especially when being entertained by an attorney from LA. Expectations were set and the green light given for the school's Principal to be interviewed for a documentary on the late, legendary Michael J. Jackson. Shortly after Principal Henry and I arrived, we observed Ms. Deborah Chang and her producer walking the school grounds marking out points of interest. Like many visiting the school where the Jackson 5 won one of their first talent shows, Ms. Chang wore the look of sheer amazement. It is a distinct look easily recognizable by locals in Gary, Indiana. Upon entering the building, Ms. Chang wasted no time actuating a stimulating conversation.

As Ms. Chang's assignment was to interview Principal Henry, I remained in the background quietly muttering Lights, Camera, Action! That day, Principal Henry shone and as her Coach and Mentor, I could not have been more proud. Ms. Chang posed intriguing questions about the learning environment, student life, school history, and of course, the school community's affection for the Jackson family. The proud Principal leading the biggest takeover school project in the state of Indiana, Ms. Henry breathlessly and eloquently answered most questions.

She paused, however, each time I interjected, "She can't answer that."

As Superintendent, it was my job to protect the integrity of the project and my school leaders, especially the Principal. Before the interview, I had already resolved that my Principal would only answer questions that directly related to school outcomes. Each interjection resulted in the interruption of production, which caused a little atmospheric tension.

After my third interjection, Ms. Chang replied, "Since you are not allowing her to answer these questions, perhaps you can."

"My pleasure," I replied.

There we were, two leaders admiring one another's strength and demeanor. Before bright lights nearly blinded me, Ms. Chang airbrushed my hair with her hand and stood back to take a good look at my seating posture. "Just start talking so that we can test your voice in the mic."

I did as directed and instantly fought back happy tears after her next statement. She said, "Gosh, you are very pretty. You look great on camera. Dr. Davis, you're a star. The camera loves you."

Was this moment real? Was I actually sitting and waiting for one of the trial attorneys who represented the mother of my favorite superstar of all time (The King of Pop) to interview me for a documentary on Michael Jackson? Yes, the moment was real. Ms. Chang and I engaged in meaningful dialogue regarding the community's affection for Michael Jackson and Mrs. Kathryn Jackson while the camera rolled.

Approximately nine months later, Ms. Chang returned to the school with Mrs. Kathryn Jackson and members of the Jackson family for a formal assembly honoring both Mrs. Jackson and the legacy of Michael Jackson. From the looks on everyone's faces, the documentary was a hit. Ms. Chang brought some Jackson-style Hollywood flair to Gary, reminding us all that dreams still come true.

Ms. Chang worked seamlessly, wrangling multi-level and multi-age groups from Gary and Los Angeles to make the program a success. At the conclusion, we embraced and she vowed to keep in touch. Promise kept. We spoke on several occasions, shedding light on each of our worlds and industries. In all of our conversations, she referred to me as a shining star. The leader in her instantly recognized the leader in me and we have esteemed one another ever since. A notable attorney with a long history of accomplishments and firsts, many would automatically assume her to be pompous and egotistical; not so. In fact, her lack of boasting combined with her compassion for others and passion for wanting to see me shine made me want to know her more intimately and introduce her as a woman who is unleashed and unafraid to lead.

Ms. Debbie Chang reigns supreme in all things "legal." A trial attorney with Panish Shea & Boyle LLP (Los Angeles) who focuses her practice on representing plaintiffs in catastrophic injury, wrongful death, and product liability cases, she has earned the respect of attorneys, judges, lawmakers, professors and aspiring attorneys.

Being a woman sweetens the pot. This "shero" is a graduate of Kansas University. Ms. Chang earned her Juris Doctorate with honors from Drake Law School, where she wasted no time applying her knowledge and skills by serving as the Case Note Editor of the Drake Law Review.

Here are a few stellar accomplishments that round out the

repertoire of this humble leader:

- ★ Named by the Daily Journal as one of the Top Women Lawyers in California for 2016 and 2017, one of the Top 100 Lawyers in California for 2017, and one of the Top Plaintiff Lawyers in California for 2017.
- ★ Received the 2014 Consumer Attorneys of California Consumer Attorney of the Year Award for her outstanding commitment to furthering the education and careers of women trial lawyers.
- ★ Brought the first lawsuit in the United States based on the newly enacted Violence Against Women Act of 1994, 42 U.S.C. § 13981 (VAWA).
- ★ Selected by the American Bar Association's Young Lawyer's Division as one of the "20 Young Lawyers Whose Work Makes a Difference" for bringing the first civil rights class action on behalf of prisoners with AIDS in a maximum security prison. The class action resulted in a landmark settlement and the formulation of model policies and procedures relating to the housing, programming and medical treatment of prisoners with AIDS currently used in prisons throughout the country.
- ★ Obtained some of the largest verdicts on record in California including the largest verdicts received in North County, San Diego (Vista) and Imperial County (El Centro).

Ms. Chang models a phrase my pastor often quotes, "Never go to battle where there are no spoils to be won."

Throughout her career, she has entered battles to win spoils that legally belong to her clients and she has mentored other women in this process. Ms. Chang's life's work teaches that it is critical to know who you are and what you can accomplish with hard work, dedication, research, and courageous action. It also teaches that you must know who and what you are fighting against and how your victory will transform the lives of others. Her legal victories have resulted in legal changes that improve lives, eradicate illegal actions toward the disenfranchised, and bring forth justice for all.

Although we are women who lead in different fields, Ms. Chang and I share commonalities. First, great leaders are not threatened by but recognize, celebrate and support other great leaders. Second, great leaders are driven by passion, purpose and the possibilities of transformation in addition to financial gain as opposed to money alone. At the end of the day, great leaders are fulfilled through accomplishing victories underpinned by a strong moral compass. Last, great leaders sustain their leadership through acts of humility, justice and service. We understand that boasting and gloating are temporal and eventually result in loss, not sustainable gain.

My leadership boldly stepped onto a higher rung after engaging with Ms. Deborah Chang. She entered my life during the winter season, literally and metaphorically. Every aspect of my work was hardened by calcified constraints, leaving my life dull and gray. This is not a great place for leaders, especially those in head positions. Encouraging myself was a bit more challenging because as I fought hard for justice for those under my tutelage, the pendulum swung harder toward injustice.

Ms. Chang's reiteration of "You're a star" during our interview for the Michael Jackson documentary reminded me that I was leading a battle with precious spoils to be won — the holistic education and development of 700+ staff and students. That was a deep revelation, for stars are lights that provide light for others, especially in times of darkness. Our interview served as a hammer to break up the cement purposely poured to block my path and obscure my view. It was as if I were the plaintiff and she my counsel. In fact, her counsel was so smooth that she provided answers and insights without asking questions that prompted trespassing on her part and treason on mine. The best part was that the smooth way in which she helped me was totally legal.

From that day, I have increased my frequency of asking leaders whom I mentor and those in my circles of influence questions that evoke reflection. As you continue or begin to embark upon your own leadership journey, reflect on these questions and make the necessary adjustments. They will help you lead your life and impact the lives of others through real humility; they will also keep you safe and legal:

- ★ What is your "Why"? Why is it important to understand why you lead?
- ★ What motivates you and drives your decision-making?
- ★ How do you stay sharp and relevant?
- ★ When do you intentionally serve those you lead? What does that look like?
- ★ To what extent are you driven by a moral compass? How do you know?
- ★ Do you follow and enforce or circumvent policies? Why?
- ★ Do you have a clear understanding of what is legal and what is not in your home/work/church/social settings?
- ★ Who mentors and/or coaches you? Do they ask questions that strengthen and deepen your leadership?

★ Who looks to you for leadership? Are you equipped to lead them to greatness? Where is your evidence?

Whatever you do, make sure you legalize your leadership. Be consistent in doing what's right whether someone is watching or not. Encourage others to do the same. And when you recognize great leadership qualities in other women, celebrate and support them. It is totally legal to esteem others, for those you esteem may be the very ones who reach back and help build a platform for you. Always remember that your life and the lives of others are greatly impacted by your decision to intentionally and courageously LEAD.

Finally, all of you, be like-minded, be sympathetic, love one another, be compassionate and humble.
(1 Peter 3:8)

Attribute 8
Familial Leadership
Ms. Laura Turner

Family is everything! The best memories from my childhood and, quite frankly, my life, are times spent with my family. Whether eating dinner on formal china with my parents, singing on the bridge with my mom, baking cookies with my dad, playing board games with my siblings and cousins, picking apples and pears from my maternal grandmother's trees, or watching westerns while chomping on pickled okra at my paternal grandparents' home, I have always loved spending quality time with family. One of the things I loved most as a teen and young adult was congregating for holidays and any occasion at the home of my Aunt Laura Turner.

Aunt Laura makes everyone feel welcomed and special. She has opened her home to family members who were homeless, jobless, motherless, and down-right hopeless. Without complaint, she'd simply gather clean linen and prepare a hearty meal. Aunt Laura personifies the scripture, *"With love and kindness have I drawn thee"* (Jeremiah 31:3b).

The oldest of 12 children, Aunt Laura now stands as the matriarch of my family from the heredity of my great-grandmother Flora Burt. Before my great-grandmother (Mama) transitioned, she boasted of her healthy lineage. I counted 104 in Chicago alone. The majority of us gathered frequently at Aunt Laura's for card games, joke sessions, memory sharing, celebrations, secret-dropping, and shooting the breeze over barbeque and soul food.

Ah, I can literally smell grilled meat mixed with watermelon and fresh cut grass from Aunt Laura's backyard. A loving host, Aunt Laura supplied and cooked a great portion of the food. She refused to allow anyone who did not bring their own food or drinks to go hungry, thirsty or ashamed. Her love and family leadership gives me hope, especially in a world where families have become more and more estranged.

One the greatest ways in which my Aunt Laura demonstrates familial leadership is by being the superglue that holds everyone together. I refer to her as "Aunt Muff with all the good stuff." Without fail, she always has good information, good conversation, good food and a good mood. Plus, I have always known her as Auntie Muff.

Like superglue, Aunt Laura possesses an amazingly humble and quiet strength that permanently connects family to family and family to God. She does not talk much, so when she does, all are attentive. We deem her words as truth filled with wisdom, for following her advice has saved our hides on many occasions. Likewise, her demonstration of unconditional love melts the stoniest hearts and bonds the toughest souls. If matters of dispute arise or rounds of damaging communication occur, they certainly dissipate after crossing Aunt Laura's threshold. In her soft sweet voice, she speaks curt words of encouragement, reminding us that none of us are perfect and we all need to ask God to help us. One of her favorite phrases is "Honey, that's not right!"

What Aunt Laura does consider right is working, owning, investing and truly living. As the eldest, she set a good example for our family. Her work resiliency is to be commended. Aunt Laura worked in the private sector for 10 years, spending two years at Styline Drapery as a receptionist and eight years the John Crerar Library at Chicago's IIT campus. Her last 31 years of formal employment were spent serving as a Medical Records Technician for U.S. Veterans Administration.

For years, I watched her leave home before the break of day to take public transportation to get to and from work. Rain, snow, sleet nor blistering heat could keep her away from fulfilling her administrative duties and serving our precious veterans. I am sure they miss her. Upon receiving her paycheck, she budgeted not only for her household but also for all who resided under her roof. I was a recipient of her generosity.

Although I was very young, I remember when Aunt Laura and her family moved from 35th & Cottage Grove to the far south side, investing in their first cozy home. What a great investment! That home would later house most of my family at some point. Aunt Laura never complained. She merely thanked God for her new home, opened her doors, provided a set of keys and invited family to attend church with her and her children. With grateful hearts, we complied.

What most of us did not know was that Aunt Laura was fulfilling the scripture: *By this shall all men know that ye are my disciples, if ye have love one to another* (John 13:35). No one questioned her followership of Jesus Christ, for it showed in everything she did even past Sunday. She was humbly leading her family through love. Through her love, we learned the value of godly relationships, home ownership and investing in self and others.

Over the past 10 years, I have participated in many funerals where people have increasingly taken the opportunity to inform everyone that their family is distant by standing during the remarks portion of the program and stating, "I'm tired of funerals being family reunions." While many can relate, I am pleased that this has not been the dominant trend for my family. Sure, there are extended relatives (younger and older) with whom I do not have a very close relationship; this does not diminish the love we share.

There were times when Aunt Laura enforced decisions as decreed by her husband — Uncle James — that I did not understand. That was when she led from the middle. All good leaders gracefully do it. Nevertheless, like friends, family members have lifestyle preferences that are not always conducive for frequent fellowship. We are there for one another, however, when it matters. There are those who choose to separate themselves because of past hurts, disagreements or plain old stubbornness. These types exist in my family, but thankfully, their choice to detach has not negatively impacted others. All it takes is one phone call from Aunt Laura or one gathering at her home to iron out disputes. She never publicly takes sides; she supports.

As a young woman, I learned much from Aunt Laura, the matriarch of my family. Aunt Laura has supported me emotionally, spiritually and financially at different times in my life. For that, I am forever grateful. Like her, her siblings (including my mother) bear a loving, fun nature derived from their mother (Laura Turner) and grandmother (Flora Burt). All are supportive, nurturing, extremely generous and a bit rough around the edges if you approach our family in an adverse way. Adopting their core values has served my family well. Many of us are grown, married and have families of our own. Because we have followed their footsteps, we find ourselves opening our hearts and homes and pouring out love to vulnerable family members. Trust me, on any given day, the barbeque grill is one match away from being fired up.

Some of the greatest lessons that I have learned from Aunt Laura's familial leadership include:

* Never give up on yourself or your family.
* Love yourself and others unconditionally.
* Love and support your spouse even if it means making decisions that family and others do not understand.
* Show tough love by confronting wrongs and seeking/giving sound counsel.
* Support and invest in yourself and those you care about.
* Boldly and lovingly share your faith.
* Always pray for your family.

My Aunt Laura is a wise and virtuous woman who leads through humility. I have always had a tender spot in my heart for her, for she has risen to the occasion and embraced her role as matriarch and serves as the model for familial leadership. I intentionally attempt to do the same. To what extent are you exhibiting familial leadership? Is it wrapped in humility? Who's following your lead?

Humble yourselves before the Lord, and he will lift you up.
(James 4:10)

Attribute Nine
Penning Leadership
Dr. Charrita D. Danley

When playwright Edward Bulwer-Lytton penned the phrase, *the pen is mightier than the sword*, he revolutionized the way the world views writers. As a teen, I wrestled to grasp the deep meaning of this statement, for my community was filled with violence and he who held the biggest knife or gun was mightier than all others (at least at that moment). Although the meaning became clear during my undergraduate years, I observed the manifestation of this powerful phrase while studying Dr. Charrita Danley for three years at Marietta High School in Marietta, Georgia.

Now the Chief of Staff to the President of Hampton University, Dr. Danley epitomizes penning leadership. In fact, her gift of writing greatly contributed to her selection as Chief of Staff. A large part of her role includes writing press releases, correspondences, speeches, reports, research papers, and grants. The uniqueness of each project necessitates succinctness and accuracy. After all, keeping a polished shine on the reputation of the President and the University takes the genius stroke of a pen in the hands of a masterful leader. At this, Dr. Danley excels, proving that *the pen is mightier than the sword*.

As Chief of Staff, Dr. Danley not only leads prestigious colleagues, but she also enjoys meaningful interactions with students in her role as advisor of the Presidential Fellows program. Dr. Danley lovingly mentors students, meeting weekly to discuss leadership, its challenges as well as rewards, and evaluate how individuals at the University and beyond exemplify it. Likewise, she engages students in book discussions on leadership topics and biographical studies of great leaders. She takes great pride in her mentees' growth and accomplishments. Truly, leading and teaching students are ingrained in the fiber of her being.

Before her promotion as the Chief of Staff, Dr. Danley played a leading role at the Georgia Department of Education and at the Georgia Professional Standards Commission (PSC) as well as served as a master teacher of high school English at Marietta High School in Marietta, Georgia. All of her positions required high-level leadership in addition to the ability to communicate effectively in writing.

My attraction to Dr. Danley came after her introduction at our English Department meeting at Marietta High School in July, 2002. She introduced herself as Charrita. The department head quickly boasted, "Dr. Charrita Danley." Intriguing! While I worked with many educators in many schools since becoming a teacher in 1995, the only educators I met who had Doctorates were Principals and Superintendents. Most were white. For the first time, I met a young, African-American teacher whose title was "Doctor." Nothing else mattered in that meeting. My goal shifted from reviewing curriculum and lesson plans to learning more about Dr. Charrita Danley.

Like most great teachers, Dr. Danley covered learning standards in creative ways and supported students in the process of acquiring and applying higher order thinking skills. Students dared not come to her class unprepared to learn and contribute. Her reputation preceded her. As African-American teachers were the minority among the teaching staff, she stood out even more. Being the new kid on the block, I sometimes used my lunch and planning periods as an opportune time to observe her classes or learn more about her educational journey, particularly her road to obtaining her Doctorate in English.

Getting a higher degree became a non-negotiable for me as I was one of three teachers who only had a Bachelor's Degree on a staff of over 50. That thought actually haunted me and provoked me to jealousy. Thankfully, Dr. Danley freely opened up and coached me through the process. Her words of encouragement and frequent check-ins propelled me to jump courageously into a graduate program. If she could do it, then I could do it.

Excitement over my new friendship had to be shared. When my mom visited me in Atlanta for the first time, I quickly introduced her to Dr. Charrita Danley. Their chemistry was evident. Before long, mom and I were spending time with Dr. Danley at her home. We even skipped Watch Service at my church to ring in the New Year with Dr. Danley at her church, New Birth Missionary Baptist Church. On our ride home, it became clear to me why mom and I were so drawn to Dr. Danley. Mom needed an editor and publisher for her new book, *New Life in Christ*. A novice to the book publishing process at the time, I could not assist mom, but Dr. Danley could. Dr. Danley laid out the process, provided publishing contact information and edited mom's first book. What a Godsend! Mom's finished product received many compliments and sales.

After helping mom through that process, Dr. Danley shared that she too would be publishing her first novel soon. Then, she made me promise not to share contents until after publishing while simultaneously handing me the raw manuscript of her acclaimed novel, *Through the Crack*. I felt so honored to be among the first to read her novel. She requested that I review it for continuity and errors and offer feedback on the overall story.

Fighting the tears was a challenge with each turn of the page. Dr. Danley's *Through the Crack* was the first novel that I read from cover to cover in one sitting. *Practically addictive* describes my first encounter with the novel.

In Danley's own words: "*Through the Crack* traces a family's journey from addiction to recovery as it exposes their individual desires to avoid being smothered by family responsibilities and relationships. The characters' faith in God sustains them through the laughter and the tears as they learn the true meaning of unconditional love."

Danley's summary can be superimposed on the complex layers of many families today, including mine. The novel's relatability drew me in so deep that I actually began to replace the characters with my own family members. The next morning, I called my uncles and aunts to tell them how much I love and appreciate them. I even called Dr. Danley to share my glowing feedback and gratitude for allowing me to serve as a first reader of *Through the Crack*.

Upon its release, *Through the Crack* scored high among readers in Atlanta. The venue where Dr. Danley held her book release and signing party was filled to capacity with eager fans. News of the release of Dr. Danley's new book traveled back to the Marietta High School community quickly. Even her students excitedly awaited their autographed copies. Their reasons for supporting their teacher were multi-faceted.

First, Dr. Danley was a teacher who modeled what she taught. Second, she and some of her students shared a similar experience: witnessing drug and alcohol use and abuse among family members and friends. Tired of reading similar stories that ended in doom and negativity, Dr. Danley decided to use her creative writing skills to address these issues, assigning a positive ending. The inspiration came from a story she witnessed that ended in recovery. She felt that such a story needed to be told. Like all good leaders, she flipped the script, turning a negative into positive with the stroke of a pen. All can gain a first-hand experience with a personal copy of *Through the Crack* available at **https://www.Amazon.com**.

Through the Crack was adapted into a play and presented by the Hampton Players and Company at Hampton University during the 2012-2013 and 2014-2015 seasons. With stellar reviews, the play is available for touring. It goes without saying that students at Hampton University love the work of Dr. Charrita Danley. What a thunderous testament to her grand leadership!

As an author, I fully appreciate Dr. Danley's creative genius. Her approach to writing and story-telling is thoughtful, courageous and intentional. After completing *Unleashed And Unafraid, Volume I*, I remember thinking to myself, "*I hope people have the same reaction I had when reading Through the Crack.*" I wanted Dr. Danley to be proud of me as well.

Both Dr. Danley and I attribute a portion of our success as creative writers and leaders to teachers and leaders we encountered as students in elementary school, high school and college, particularly our English teachers. Their inspiring teachings and tactical guidance opened our eyes to new worlds through literature and taught us how to think critically about texts and the world in which we live. They also nurtured our love of language and enhanced our writing skills through instruction. Because of the tremendous impact our teachers had on us, we have both developed a strong desire to touch the lives of young people, leading them to their greatness.

I mention many of my beloved teachers in *Unleashed And*

Unafraid, Volume I in the chapter "Teach." Due to the excellent teaching and leadership Dr. Danley's teachers provided, it is befitting that they be honored here by name: Mrs. Verna Parham, Mrs. Shirley Walker Cartlidge, Ms. Jacqueline Liddell McWilliams, Ms. Victoria Hall, and Dr. Jerry W. Ward, Jr.

Dr. Danley's life is an obvious manifestation of the biblical principle, *"A man's gift makes room for him, and brings him before great men."* (Proverbs 18:16). She is humbly using her gifts of writing and leading to guide her own life and have an impact on the leadership and lives of others. Both are being accomplished through the stroke of the literal and electronic pen.

What instruments are you using to lead your own life? How are they working for you? To what extent do you use them to aid in the learning of others?

Let us not become weary in doing good, for at the proper time we will reap a harvest if we do not give up.
(Galatians 6:9)

Attribute Ten
Persevering Leadership
Ms. Carolyn Mack

A well-known and often rehearsed scripture states *"The race is not given to the swift nor the strong, but he who endures to the end"* (Ecclesiastes 9:11). The revelation of this scripture points to perseverance. Women of excellence who intentionally lead their lives understand the value and benefits of perseverance. Consider the analogy of a runner. The runner may be swift, but if she does not finish the race, she will not meet her goal and cannot claim victory. Similarly, if a runner is stronger than her competitors but does not finish her race, she too will not meet her goal and can in no wise claim victory. The victory can only be claimed by those who persevere and finish the race. Such runners run to win. Leaders, who persevere, lead to win. Such is the case with Ms. Carolyn Mack.

Ms. Mack and I met at the Ultimate Women's Expo in Los Angeles. We were both there to discover a hidden treasure — one another. Totally exhilarated from delivering my first Women's Expo Seminar on the main stage, I strolled back to my booth. Many women were waiting to purchase autographed copies of *Unleashed And Unafraid, Volume I*; some were waiting to tell me how my talk on being unleashed and unafraid lit fire under their feet; others wanted to hug me. What all needed was a touch from the God in me. Mission accomplished. After embracing the last woman, I finally gave my feet a rest.

Before long, I was up again listening to a woman who seemingly appeared from nowhere. She was modestly dressed and wore a charming smile. Her handshake was strong yet genteel and her words were poetic. She complimented my appearance and spirit of excellence. Her third sentence blew me away. She said, "Let me introduce myself. My name is Carolyn Mack. God told me that you are to play a role in my movie. God told me, 'Get her.'"

An actress, her words were music to my ears. I had not come to Los Angeles hoping to be "discovered by Hollywood." My goal was to advance my Unleashed And Unafraid Movement through the delivery of my live seminar, engagement with expo attendees and sale of books. God had other plans. Ms. Mack and I exchanged contact information, embraced and vowed to reconnect.

Months later, Ms. Mack called to share the details of her movie project. Her high level of excitement stirred my soul. I thought to myself, "If she is this excited over me accepting a minor role, this is definitely a divine connection." What I did not know was that from the time of our introduction to the time of the phone call, God had shifted my position. Ms. Mack went on to reveal that when God told her *"Get her,"* He actually meant "she is your lead female actress for your movie." In slow motion, my cell phone slipped out of my hand and a happy tear rolled down my right cheek. After 40 years of waiting for a second chance and five years after *spying out the land,* I received a call from Ms. Mack of Hollywood.

Two worlds converged, led by two women who had persevered and refused to allow age and circumstances to dictate their courses. Just as I had waited 40 years to receive another call from Hollywood, Ms. Mack had waited more than 40 years to write, direct and produce her first big movie. At 60+ years, she dared to publicize her dream boldly. She had not given up on implementing her vision. Nor had she stopped persevering in the face of adversity.

When Ms. Mack relocated from North Carolina to Hollywood, she did not have a Plan B. Like all great leaders, she took the courage and put a laser focus on her vision, implementing a strategic plan to bring her vision (dream) to life. A woman of great integrity, Ms. Mack bore realistic expectations in the land of dreams. She knew the possibility of her dream manifesting overnight was slim, but she persevered through the setbacks and frustrations. She devised her own professional development plan to learn about script writing and producing. Frequenting workshops, festivals, and writing events became her new norm. Despite her age, she even interned for a respected Hollywood producer.

Imagine my expression when learning Ms. Mack's age. The expression was a blend of amazement and glee. At a time when I nearly relinquished my 40-year dream of acting, God connected me with Ms. Mack to shut my mouth and teach me a lesson in leadership perseverance. Marriage of the two resonated as a new concept. The revelation and timing of my meeting Ms. Mack became clearer with each conversation. Details of my life show that I am no stranger to persevering. What I and others need to learn is how to lead our lives through perseverance. Ms. Mack's life has proven that there is a difference.

Leading through persevering requires a fortified mindset that disallows abandonment of vision and mission even if offered easier paths or better choices. When Ms. Mack said she did not have a Plan B, she was essentially saying that she had chosen a race to run and she would not only finish, but win. She chose to lead her life her way in the face of disillusionment, determining that she would achieve her dream despite stage, age and the perceptions of others. Take that!

Ms. Mack's leadership and perseverance are paying off. She is the writer, producer and director of the film *A Way With Anger*. *A Way With Anger* is a powerful film about forgiveness. In Ms. Mack's words, *"The film will be used as a tool for The Forgiveness Movement to reach the masses."* As a leading actress in the film, I agree. Reading the script forced me to deal with areas of un-forgiveness for which I was unaware. Healing became my portion as I delved deeper into my character. After several readings, I had a greater understanding of selective perseverance. I was also compelled to re-evaluate relationships that I was ready to sever due to the residue of un-forgiveness.

Ms. Mack ranks high on my list of heroines. Her ability to lead through perseverance is rare at this point in history for someone who has not yet "made it" by societal standards, especially at her age. Instead of laying aside her life, she is intentionally leading her life and impacting the lives she touches. Today, Ms. Mack is living her dream. Her life serves as a model for all those who dare unapologetically to live out their purpose. Correspondently, notable producers now approach her to partner on major television projects and web series. She understands that she has been created to lead a movement through the arts that will change lives. That understanding resonates with me. For that, she will be revered as she continues to lead and persevere.

What about you? Make the choice to lead your life intentionally and find fulfillment in persevering through the process. You won't regret it!

What, then, shall we say in response to these things? If God is for us, who can be against us?
(Romans 8:31)

Attribute 11
Heart Leadership
Mrs. Veriner James

Respected leaders possess character-building attributes that serve them well in popular and unpopular situations. Punking out is never an option. Sometimes, when great leaders are being made, they are rough around the edges and a bit stubborn in times of agreeing. Neither should be mistaken for open rebellion. Unfortunately, this is the very case when other "leaders" do not take the time to understand the Heart of leadership. I have come to understand that in order to lead your life, it is imperative to have "Heart." This brings me to a woman of excellence who has mastered the art of leading with heart — Mrs. Veriner James.

Upon meeting Mrs. James, I knew I was in the presence of a chosen one. Every student who decided to work beneath his/her potential dreaded being enrolled in Mrs. James' English class. They understood that their days of turning in half-completed work on wrinkled, fringed paper for grade consideration were over. Likewise, every teacher who had the idea of writing lesson plans and teaching half-heartedly wished they had a different lead teacher.

Even Administrators were sometimes taken aback by her courageous approach to sensitive situations. It was directly, and sometimes indirectly, made clear to all that she demanded excellence absent negotiation. In many respects, watching her was like surveying me as a young teacher. Early in the game, she learned to take calculated risks. She had Heart.

Leaders who lead with heart make bold, yet sometimes unpopular decisions. Leaders with heart also influence others. Mrs. James epitomizes these concepts. The ability to enact both smoothly is what I admire most about Mrs. James. Undoubtedly, these attributes will serve her well as Founder and Head of School of the Exousia Leadership Academy for Girls (Chicago, Illinois). On occasion, I have observed Mrs. James fervently communicate her perspective and defend her decisions in leadership meetings around school-related issues including student discipline, class/homework policies, and effective grading practices. Although some disagreed, all actively listened and reflected.

I met Mrs. James during our two-week in-service and training for our take-over school project in Gary in 2012. She was hired by the new Principal in the role of Lead Teacher for the 11th & 12th Grade-Level Team. Mrs. James and I did not engage much (on a personal level) until an issue arose between she and an administrator and I was asked to provide guidance. As one of the Directors of Achievement appointed to coach the Principal and support the Leadership Team, the request was not unreasonable.

The dispute centered on student attendance and grades. Mrs. James was unrelenting in her position that students who have excessive absences should not receive passing grades. First, many students could not prove mastery (or in some instances a basic understanding) of the material she covered in class. Long gone were the days where effort set the standard. Second, spending time grading student work that was incomplete or poorly presented was not worth her time.

Her position was not popular or favored. Mrs. James knew exactly where she worked, and students' history of failure(s), yet she was unrelenting, insisting that students meet her class expectations in order to pass. Likewise, the team was unyielding on its stance to give students a break because of the failure they experienced under the previous administration. As I listened to this fascinating leadership dilemma, I saw an opportunity and was instantly impressed with Mrs. James' ability to take such a calculated risk by respectfully fighting for what she believed was morally right. This "chess move" took Heart.

Things could have ended unfavorably for Mrs. James. Instead, this dilemma influenced a major shift, accelerating a training that my colleague, Annie Baddoo, and I planned to facilitate later in the school year: Effective Grading Practices. Essential components of the on-going training included the purpose, value, and commitment to implement effective grading practices school-wide in order to improve student performance in all classes.

This would not be my last observation of Mrs. James leading with heart. Whether engaging with school leaders, colleagues, students and/or parents, Mrs. James remained consistent. She fought many tough battles; her heart never failed. One of the toughest decisions I watched her make was to decide whether or not to change a student's grade from an "F" to a "D," which would have made the student eligible to graduate. The student received passing grades in all classes but hers and the weight of the decision to graduate the student was suddenly on her shoulder.

She took heart and put the weight back on the shoulders of the student, explaining that the decision was made the moment the student decided not to meet requirements. Hearts were broken, including hers, but leaders who lead their lives understand that heartbreak is sometimes a byproduct of the process. That day, Mrs. James made more than a tough decision. She showed the very essence and importance of leading with "Heart." The student graduated a few months later, after successfully completing summer school.

Approximately one month after this memorable occurrence, I received a phone call from a recruiter regarding Mrs. James' ability to lead a school in the capacity of Principal. I remember that call as if it had taken place yesterday. As a Superintendent who supported Principals and knew what a strong Principal looked like, I was happy to provide my response: "Yes, she is!"

When asked "Why," I stated:

"Mrs. James is ready to lead her own school because she leads with HEART. She leads courageously, equipped with knowledge, understanding and wisdom of education reform and its impact on vulnerable students. She also leads with a heart of compassion. She cares about the educational attainment, spiritual growth and social-emotional needs of inner-city kids. In fact, the moral compass of her heart holds her and her students to high expectations, understanding that it takes a combination of grit, determination, love and patience to achieve in school and in life. She knows the urgency around helping students achieve and she is relentless in her approach to help students and teachers excel."

A few days later, Mrs. James called me to share the good news. She was appointed to her first Principalship. Feelings of elation raced through me as I listened to her share her excitement. I knew having "Heart" would pay off for her. And, I knew she needed "Heart" to Principal an alternative school in one of

Chicago's toughest communities. With a heart for God, a heart for His children and the "Heart" to be more than a conqueror, Mrs. James excelled. Under her leadership, some of Chicago's most vulnerable students finally graduated high school and now have a start at life; increased test scores gained the attention of top leaders in Chicago; and teachers improved.

Today, Mrs. James is preparing to open the Exousia Leadership Academy for Girls, a private school for girls in Chicago proper. This accomplishment puts her on the platform with the late, great Educator Extraordinaire, Marva Collins. Mrs. James truly leads her life with "Heart" and all of the girls of Exousia will greatly benefit as a result. With a supportive husband, son, and family by her side, Mrs. James will keep soaring. She is a champion in multiple respects who understands the trans-generational benefits and value of leading with "Heart."

What about you?

So do not fear, for I am with you;
do not be dismayed, for I am your God.
I will strengthen you and help you;
I will uphold you with my righteous right hand.
(Isaiah 41:10)

Attribute 12
Profound Leadership
Ms. Sabrina Valdez

In William Shakespeare's play, *Romeo and Juliet*, Juliet asks a question that scholars have examined for centuries: "What's in a name?" Some argue that young Juliet displayed wisdom in understanding that it is not the name but the character of a person that matters. Others argue that Juliet revealed her youthful ignorance for asking this question, for it has been understood since the beginning of humanity that names are very important as they symbolize a person's identity. Fascinated by names and their meanings, especially my own, I can easily make a case for each argument. Like character, names are an essential aspect of identity. Observations reveal that people display actions in accordance with the meaning of their names. Because names embody the essence of a person, all should choose names carefully. Thankfully, my mother named me *Sabrena*. My father affirmed my identity.

In some cultures, the name *Sabrina* means legendary princess or royal child. In others, *Sabrina* means beyond the boundary or from the border. Fleshed out, these meanings characterize *Sabrina* as a royal princess who lives on the edge, going beyond boundaries venturing into the world where human perception wilts. Without delving deeper into etymologies and derivations, I can surely attest that this description perfectly depicts Ms. Sabrina

Valdez, Executive Pastor at Sendero Life Center (Moses Lake, Washington) and John Maxwell Speaker, Coach and Trainer.

Upon meeting her on my first day at the John Maxwell Live Certification Training Event, I knew that Ms. Sabrina was of *"a royal priesthood, a holy nation, God's special possession..."* (I Peter 2:9 NIV). Her regal vivacity immediately caught my attention. I was attracted to it because it exists within me. With enthusiasm, we spoke, embraced and engaged in genuine conversation. When she shared that her name was Sabrina, in a high-pitched voice, I cheerfully said, "Oh my God. I knew there was something extra special about you. Sabrina, meet Sabrena."

There we were, two royal princesses sent by God to venture into the world of ultimate spiritual and natural leadership to gain the tools needed to lead our lives and influentially impact the lives of those we serve. Both Ms. Sabrina and I had studied the leadership work of John C. Maxwell years before attending the Live Certification Event. Learning from the #1 leadership guru in the world (along with other phenomenal JMT Leaders) in a face-to-face setting was amazing. More than anything, our spirits were determined to *"hear counsel, and receive instruction, [to be wise] in [our] latter end"* (Proverbs 19:20). Our time had come to go beyond the boundaries of our own leadership. Our time had come to join the ranks of prolific leaders known for changing their worlds. As the meaning of our names suggests, we had humbly yielded to God's will to go boldly where we had never traveled before. Key learning from the event certainly had a profound effect on our lives.

Like most princesses, Ms. Sabrina felt a call to leadership and ministry at a young age, 12 to be exact. Neither timidity nor shyness could stop her from fulfilling this special call. Whether consciously or subconsciously, she clutched the significance of the number 12. Since biblical days, there has been a strong correlation between the number 12 and leadership: Jesus questioned scholars in the temple at age 12; there were 12 tribes of Jacob who formed the 12 tribes of Israel. There were 12 judges of Israel; Jesus identified 12 disciples who later became the 12 Apostles. Jesus healed the woman who had an issue of blood for 12 years; and Revelations 21:12 states that the New Jerusalem will have 12 gates guarded by 12 angels. Like her biblical predecessors, Ms. Sabrina transcends the notion of the perfect 10 and resides in the realm of the prolific 12. The fruit of her labor is tangibly evident.

As a young leader, Ms. Sabrina had a heart for people and a passion for missions. At age 16, her inner leader motioned her to travel to Ghana, Africa. She journeyed alongside other young leaders with the Teen Mania organization. That profound experience forever changed her life. After returning home, she became very active within her youth group at church. The roots of leadership undoubtedly began to anchor themselves deep in her spirit. Upon graduating high school, her leadership and influence ramped up. Ms. Sabrina felt compelled to attend Phoenix First Pastors College to expand her knowledge base and dive deeper into leadership. Her new road led to an internship with the campus Bus Ministry. Life and leadership were about to get a bit more interesting.

Unleashed and unafraid, Ms. Sabrina traveled to the roughest parts of downtown Phoenix, Arizona transporting children, teens, impoverished adults, drug dealers, and prostitutes to church. She crossed the border and stepped up to be the conduit between two different worlds. Totally prolific! What a perfect example of a familiar scripture, *"And the Lord said unto the servant, Go out into the highways and hedges, and compel them to come in, that my house may be filled"* (Luke 14:23).

Ms. Sabrina used her love for people and her impactful influence to lead those most vulnerable to Christ and a life of freedom. (Similarly, I evangelized door to door in the projects every Sunday morning, ministering to a similar demographic of people. In both instances, lives were changed). Then God tapped on Ms. Sabrina's shoulders again, calling her to a higher level of leadership. This time, He used one of her mentoring leaders to introduce her to one of John C. Maxwell's books, *The 360° Leader*. One profound quote from the book states, "Great people talk about ideas, average people talk about themselves, and small people talk about others." This revelation catapulted Ms. Sabrina to a higher leadership domain.

A young leader who focused on big ideas since the age of 12, Ms. Sabrina discovered a niche. She got hooked, often going to a second-hand bookstore to buy other books written by John Maxwell. Although she was not in a formal leadership position at the time, she knew God was instructing her to keep studying the principles of leadership for the future. Through her readings, she began to grow a mentality that leadership is not a position or title and that we are all called to lead, whether in our homes, close circles, communities or places of work. This prolific leader not only talks the talk but also walks that walk. Our strides bear much similarity.

Ms. Sabrina and I not only share first names, we share a passion for keeping our leadership iron-sharp through both leading and serving. We are women after God's heart and we have become what Maxwell refers to as the 360° Leader. We have learned to lead ourselves, lead those under our tutelage, and influence those above us. This is how we get things done and make meaningful impact in our worlds. We share a testimony that God empowers women to make a difference in His kingdom and in the world; there are no barriers to what He can do through us. All is done through humility, understanding that no matter how passionate and skilled we are, God is first in everything. In fact, Ms. Sabrina lives by a quote housed on her Facebook page, "I AM

SECOND." Only a humble, wise leader would dare publicly post such a profound statement. In her own words,

> *"'I AM SECOND' is such a simple statement but yet so profound. Since the moment that I read it, it has gripped me to the point that it has become my life's goal. It's a statement that one must live out daily. It's declaring that God is first in everything that I am a part of and I am to remain second. This statement is living out a change of lifestyle; it is one that each Christian should possess and even more, leaders. To be second, one must be humble and recognize she is not in control. To be second requires that one follows behind the main leader, God Himself."*

As the Executive Pastor at Sendero Life Center, Ms. Sabrina Valdez supports the Senior Pastor in implementing the church's vision; creates structures and systems that allow her and the church staff to execute the vision and mission; supervises staff in ways that maximize ministry effectiveness; and works with the church Board to manage facilities. She enhanced her ability to effectively lead others and produce excellence through her "Ministry in Leadership" studies at Northwest University where she earned her Bachelor's Degree.

A 2018 graduate, Ms. Sabrina Valdez epitomizes a passionate, prolific leader. Her leadership results in productivity, creativity and fruit and has a profound effect on all those around her. One need only view the Sendero Life Center website to see the value of her (and her team's) leadership. Ms. Sabrina is on fire. Don't even think about trying to extinguish her flame. God just turned up the heat and she is sparking flames prolifically with no plan of slowing down. The same is true for me.

What about you? How hot is your flame? In what ways have you sharpened your leadership lately? Do you have a passion for leading and supporting others? What profound effect does your leadership have on others?

It's time to be like the Sabrinas/Sabrenas of the world: trust God and let Him lead you beyond your borders to a whole new world where you *live and love to lead*. The masses are waiting!

Don't let anyone look down on you because you are young, but set an example for the believers in speech, in conduct, in love, in faith and in purity.
(1 Timothy 4:12)

Attribute Thirteen
Pharmaceutical Leadership
Dr. Briancca Marshall

In most cultures, staring can be associated with rude or hostile behavior, especially if the object of affection is one with whom the observer is not acquainted. Many people stare subconsciously, unaware of their conduct thereby oblivious to its effect. Contrarily, many stare as a result of a person's or object's beauty, uniqueness, horridness or dissimilarity. Remarkably, my vast experiences in leadership have led me to conclude that there is a greater purpose revealed by subconscious staring that transcends physical attributes. That greater purpose centers on engaged connectedness.

Whenever I facilitate a workshop or seminar, automaticity occurs. Without warning, my eyes automatically scan the room, becoming fixated on certain individuals with whom I find myself both pleasurably engaged and connected throughout the workshop. Similarly, when traveling, I find myself staring at certain people to the point of discomfort. Thankfully, this experience doesn't happen frequently. When I become aware of my seemingly rude behavior, I take action and prudently approach the person. Failure to do so may result in a missed opportunity to engage with someone with whom I am ordained to connect. Thankfully, the leader in me did not fail on a frosty

December day.

Dr. Briancca Marshall and I exchanged glances and smiles multiple times while waiting to board our plane at Chicago's Midway Airport. She had a very pleasant demeanor. I found myself staring at her as we sat awaiting the boarding process in Chicago and as we waited for the rental car shuttle at the Reagan National Airport in DC. Who knows what thoughts she contemplated as she caught my eyes each time? Finally, as we sat in neighboring seats, I initiated a conversation that would result in the inclusion of Dr. Briancca in *Unleashed And Unafraid, Volume II.*

In our conversation, I learned that Dr. Briancca and I had much in common. In some ways, it was as if I were speaking to a younger me. Humility, ambition, determination, love, giving and excellence all came to mind as she shared tidbits of her upbringing, educational journey, and current work. It is not often that I meet well-rounded, successful Millennials who walk in true humility, especially in leadership. Nothing about Dr. Briancca's demeanor or conversation spelled pride or egoism. Quite refreshing! When asked her occupation, she shared she was a Pharmacist. Upon asking her to clarify whether she said Pharmacist or Pharmacy Tech. She replied, "Pharmacist." At that moment, my purpose for staring became clear.

Honestly, I had never met a young, black, female Pharmacist before making acquaintance with Dr. Briancca. I felt like a proud big sister. Although our bus ride was short, I managed to gather all the information I could in an effort to peek into her life. Asking the right questions was pivotal: What motivated you to become a Pharmacist? What college did you attend and to what extent did the program prepare you for your job? What challenges did you face? What path did you take to earn your PharmD, and how long did it take you to earn your Doctorate? Her responses provoked deep reflection in addition to a renewed commitment to intentionally guide our next generation of leaders.

Here is what Dr. Briancca Marshall shared:

"I knew that I wanted to be a pharmacist around my sophomore year of high school. My motivation was my father. He had high blood pressure and was always taking his medication, which initially got me interested. I would look at his medications with him and ask questions about what they were for, when he was supposed to take them and how they worked. High blood pressure is serious and he had it for a while so medications became my passion. I would make sure he was taking them, go with him to the pharmacy to pick them up, and talk to the pharmacists about my father's medications."

Engaging in this personalized process led Dr. Briancca to enroll in an eight-week collaborative program between the University of Illinois at Chicago and CVS Pharmacy, specifically designed for high school students. While successfully completing the program, she solidified her decision and began preparing for pharmacy school. After graduating from Chicago's prestigious Whitney Young High School, Dr. Briancca enrolled at Howard University where she completed all the prerequisites for admission to Howard's College of Pharmacy. Normally, it takes two to four years for undergraduate students to complete prerequisites, but Dr. Briancca was so determined to make a difference in the lives of her family and community that she completed all required courses in two years. Admission to Howard's prestigious graduate College of Pharmacy granted!

A few years later, Ms. Briancca Marshall would be introduced to the world as Dr. Briancca Marshall (Briancca Marshall, PharmD.). Her outstanding education from Howard University, a prestigious and high ranking Historically Black College & University, earned her a space among Chicago

Pharmacists. Thankfully, her father pressed his way to see Dr. Briancca earn her PharmD before he transitioned. That sentimental moment is a highlight in her life.

Often mistaken for a Pharmacy Tech due to her age and humble spirit, Dr. Briancca serves as a great role model for others who wish to lead in the medical field but do not wish to become medical doctors. She is a preceptor for current pharmacy students from the University of Illinois at Chicago. Moreover, she mentors and tutors high school students who are interested in the pharmaceutical field. She gives students a realistic look into the daily operations of pharmacy: filling prescriptions, speaking to doctors, providing consultations, checking patients' blood pressure and providing them with loads of information. Because of her father's experience with hypertension, Dr. Briancca is very passionate about educating patients about hypertension. She goes the extra mile by outlining lifestyle modifications, including diet and exercise, after sharing her personal family history.

Although work keeps her busy, Dr. Briancca makes time to educate students in Chicago high schools about the endless possibilities of going to college, focusing on career paths in the field of pharmacy. When visiting D.C., Dr. Briancca speaks to students enrolled at Howard University's College of Pharmacy to encourage and motivate them. Many recognize her as a passionate mentor from the Pharmacy Initiative Leaders Program.

Dr. Briancca and I began our outward leadership journeys as resilient teens determined to change the trajectory of our families and dedicated to our life's work. She began pharmacy school at 19 and earned her Doctor of Pharmacy Degree at 24 while I began teaching and evangelizing within my family and community at eight and began teaching high school at 22. Our accomplishments were underpinned by our willingness to remain humble and lead with the purpose of positively affecting the lives of others.

These represent characteristics of great leaders. Dr. Briancca's leadership reveals that the work of PharmDs is just as important as the work of MDs, for while MDs make diagnoses based on research that saves lives, PharmDs ensure correct doses of medications that sustain lives. My leadership reveals that the work of EdDs (Educational Doctors) are critical for sustaining and advancing of society, for everyone in every field needs educating. Every doctor, lawyer, scientist, entrepreneur, musician, etc. encountered some form of formal education (in a classroom, homeschool or online) in order to gain the skills and practice needed to hone their crafts and build their financial futures.

Our combined leadership demonstrates that one is never too young to lead and one's age, race and socio-economic status do not determine one's success as a leader. It is one's humility, determination, willingness to take calculated risks and intentional acts of giving back that identifies one as a leader. Allow nothing to deter you from intentionally leading your own life, especially people, circumstances and controlled substances. As I state in most of my live seminars, people do not understand your vision because God gave it to you not them; yield your will to God's and lead through His strength. Humble yourself so God doesn't have to. The only drug you should ever take to get high is a good dose of the Holy Ghost.

Get a coach and/or mentor to help you. All great leaders have coaches. And remember, take the courage to lead your life intentionally in ways that bless you and impact those around you. Take the right leadership medicine (*character, courage, discipline, excellence, faith, genuineness, hard work, honesty, hope, integrity, optimism, quality, responsibility, visibility, wisdom, and zealousness*) and the right doses for optimal success. This prescription is extracted from Dr. Briancca Marshall's and my life with the approval of our Father God. Now, go and lead Unleashed And Unafraid!

*The plans of the diligent lead to profit
as surely as haste leads to poverty.*
(Proverbs 21:5)

Attribute 14
Disruptive Leadership
Ms. Leia Avery

At the cutting edge of the gaming industry stands a lovely, innovative leader whose entrepreneurial techniques are alluringly savvy. Just over 30, Ms. Leia Avery is unapologetically disrupting the board game industry. She is leading a trans-generational movement that stimulates laughter, promotes healthy competition, strengthens relationships, enhances creativity and decreases stress. Even first-timers and non-gamers get hooked quickly and engage often in Ms. Avery's signature Just Play events. She has totally flipped boredom on its head, disrupting the way Americans party on Friday nights.

My introduction of Ms. Avery came by way of school technology specialist Desmond DeBardlebon. On lunch breaks, we discussed creative, human-centered solutions to world problems. After sharing my idea for a new game concept, Mr. DeBardlebon asked if I had made acquaintance with Leia Avery. Her name surfaced often at the Chicago Black Inventors meetings I attended, but acquaintance had not yet occurred. That reflection along with Mr. DeBardlebon's inquiry incited exploration.

At the conclusion of the first call, a decision was rendered. Ms. Leia Avery unquestionably fit the description of a woman of excellence who leads her life. Intrigued by her journey as a young inventor and Founder of Just Play Entertainment, Inc., I was eager to understand her entrepreneurial mindset and inventive process.

Images of leadership and disruption formed as she spoke. A student and champion of *Disruptive Innovation*, I know a disrupter by the threading of her ideas.

Like all pure disrupters, Ms. Avery is what Malcolm Gladwell (renowned author of *The Tipping Point*) refers to as a creative, conscientious, and disagreeable entrepreneur. There exists a substantial body of research about disruptive innovation. Among the easiest definitions to comprehend is "Disruptive Innovation" found on Wikipedia. Accordingly, *"Disruptive innovation refers to an innovation that creates a new market and value network and eventually disrupts an existing market and value network."*

("Disruptive Innovation." Wikipedia. Wikipedia.org. ***https://en.wikipedia.org/wiki/Disruptive_innovation***. Accessed March 23, 2018).

The work of Ms. Leia Avery aligns perfectly with this description. Her establishment of the Just Play Entertainment Company has indeed created a new market and value network. The invention and introduction of Ms. Avery's signature game, Hip Hop Charades, has interrupted the flow of the current board game industry and captured the engagement of gamers in a whole new realm. The value network organically produced demands respect. The fun doesn't stop here. In addition to producing games, Just Play Entertainment hosts Just Play events in major cities featuring other games inventors, where teams compete to win championship titles in a variety of games.

Moreover, the company customizes gameplay for themed parties such as Bridal Jeopardy, Office Feud, and Sweet 16. Individuals and organizational teams benefit from active participation in Ms. Avery's monthly game night events via *Just Play Ministries* for churches, *Just Play Academy* for schools, *Just Play Corporate* for companies, and Hip Hop Charades Lunch Break

Rounds on Facebook. For app fans, Ms. Avery has created the Hip Hop Charades eGame. Gamers can play her popular game via smartphone, tablet or smart TV with different categories including I Love the 90s, Pop Culture, Naughty Charades and much more.

Those blessed to attend the Atlanta Black Women's Expo can now participate in Ms. Avery's Entrepreneurial Workshop titled *Entrepreneurship – The Untold part of the Game*. The objective of the workshop is to highlight unforeseen challenges and provide strategies to help build better business practices. Unquestionably, Ms. Avery strategically designs interactive experiences by providing a diverse set of values attracting new markets often overlooked by existing gaming giants.

A notably sentimental accomplishment for Ms. Avery is assisting her dad with the packaging and components of his Obama-Mania board game. The Obama-Mania board game made history when decision-makers at the DuSable Museum of African-American History in Chicago took interest and stocked the game for sale. What a proud moment for this father-daughter team. Not only has she assisted her father, Ms. Avery has countlessly advised aspiring game inventors on the manufacturing and sales process. In fact, Just Play is currently launching a brand ambassador program to train others in different cities to host their own Just Play Events. What a bold move for a classy leader!

While current ideology continues to grapple with the longstanding axiom that leaders are born, of Ms. Avery's leadership, I assert that she was born and has been made to lead. At a young age, a stirring for leadership surfaced. She observed her father manage all aspects of a popcorn shop in Chicago. Enjoying the tasty treat while learning from her father, Ms. Avery entertained sweet thoughts of entrepreneurship. While attending Tennessee State University, she opened and operated both a popcorn shop and a music kiosk in a mall in Nashville. Both proved successful. History reveals that Ms. Avery has always been on the cutting edge of disruptive leadership, driven by her purpose and passion to entertain adults in ways that result in distressing and enjoying healthy moments of fun.

Similar to Ms. Avery, I have been known to introduce disruptive innovations in my line of work. My most recent revolves around metric systems for takeover schools. Metric systems are not new; however, the value attributed to takeover schools established by existing metric systems does not adequately reveal school improvement progress. Alternatively, most metrics, established before improvement plans often reveal a lack of progress. This tendency lends itself to unfairness and bias. Not willing to accept this inequity, I introduced a different set of metrics for which to measure real progress. The value-add produced a wow effect. My school team and I identified takeovers as a new market that required a whole new set of metrics to gauge success.

When tested against my newly metric system, contractual measures were met and we had much to celebrate. Results revealed significant progress and a higher state grade than the state grade as gauged by the inequitable metric system used by states. Understanding the inevitable pushback, I took the courage to introduce this disruptive idea as I knew it had significant implications on our strategic work and would greatly impact our bottom line. After all, I was the leader with a strong moral compass unmoved by what others thought where my staff and students were concerned. The innovation was not accepted immediately, but it proved true in the end. That's leadership.

Ms. Leia Avery possesses the unique ability to give life to innovations that disrupts status quo while positively impacting others. Her ability was not acquired by accident. It resulted from discipline and a laser focus on her business model for Just Play

Entertainment. Like most great leaders, she understands that business comes first while fun follows.

Much can be learned from this young disruptor's life. She is not only leading her life, but she is paving the way for those who dare to be conscientious and bold enough to live creatively and construct what does not exist. So am I. We are living proof that disruptive leadership is vital to life — personal and professional. One must not be afraid to lead her life in a disruptive manner, especially when repeated actions do not yield desired results. The time has come to entertain new ideas, do things differently and lead your life with no regard to the pessimistic views of others. Create your own opportunities and stop waiting for someone else to open doors for you.

As a dear friend strongly admonished before getting his wings, "Do it yourself!" Disrupt what has been disrupting you and start leading your life.

She is clothed with strength and dignity;
she can laugh at the days to come.
(Proverbs 31:25)

Attribute 15
Tailor-MADE Leadership
Mrs. Valdavia Ellis

Have you ever put on a pair of jeans that made your spirit sing? What about slipping into a dress that made you feel like the most dazzling woman on earth? Each time I slide into my jeans designed by fashion designers Valdavia & Stacey Ellis, song lyrics to Bruno Mar's "Uptown Funk" and the Commodores' "Brickhouse" start singing in my head causing me to joyously parade in front of my mirror. Who knew jeans could make you sing?

My jeans are perfectly tailored to cuddle every curve. I am so attractive to myself that when I gaze in the mirror, the only thing I see is God's beautiful creation. That's by design, for the couple's mission is to show people the love of God by clothing them with love specifically designed for their bodies. Such love allows us to see how God looks at us and reflect on the purpose for which we were all MADE. Clients quickly realize that putting on clothes designed and tailor-made with love lifts their spirits from the inside out. What a fresh perspective!

The Co-CEOs of House of MADE, Ms. Valdavia and Mr. Stacey Ellis are Fashion Designers and the Inventors of the patented curved fit system for denim jeans and fashion who understand how to tailor garments that flatter every body. The key to their success is rooted in the understanding for the purpose of clothing dating back to the Garden of Eden. Summarizing Ms. Val, *God expressed an act of love by making clothes for Adam and Eve before sending them out of the garden. The clothes were designed to fit their unique bodies [and conform to the elements]. God made the best for His best creation. Thus, our inspiration for using our patented technology to design and make clothes sized for every body type.* Amazing!

I met Ms. Val and Stacey at the wedding of a darling mutual friend, Ms. Nicole Jackson. Nicole invited me to a "Jean Party" prior to the wedding, but a previously scheduled engagement resulted in my declination. Party pictures posted on Facebook evoked curiosity. That was nothing compared to what I observed in person when Ms. Val and Stacey entered the venue. A stunning couple, they captured everyone's attention. I secretly hoped they were seated at my table. They were.

Upon reaching the table, Stacy proceeded to remove Ms. Val's flowing swing coat revealing the "baddest" winter dress I had ever seen: a long, fitted, blue and black, slim-waist A-liner with accented leather sleeves. She and her dress were one. At an appropriate time, I introduced myself and engaged her in small talk only to learn that she was the designer of all the jeans women proudly modeled in Nichole's Facebook posts.

"Where did you get that lovely dress?" I asked.

"Oh, I made it" she replied with a smile. Noticing the marvel on my face, her husband grinned, gave me a card and told me to come by the studio for a fitting. A week later, my mom and I showed up for our scheduled visit and got so much more.

The door opened and there stood the beautifully liberated Ms. Val decked out in a two-piece, alluring, self-tailored denim outfit with complementing three-inch heels. Just as before, my jaw dropped and my head bobbled in sheer amazement. Magazine models were no match for this gorgeous genius. Ms. Val embraced us then sashayed to the center of the studio. Her poise and confidence were indisputable. She was truly the leading lady.

Before our fitting, Ms. Val and Stacey took the liberty to share their passion for the art and science of making people look and feel good. An experienced educator, I was no stranger to looking through the lenses of art and science to teach varying concepts. But, the art and science of designing clothes had never crossed my mind. When the couple shared that they had invented and patented a technological formula for tailoring clothes, I got comfortable on the sofa and prepared myself for a life lesson. With their combined degrees in Science & Technology and Fashion Design, these Howard University Alums positioned themselves to tailor-make their own empire and rule in multiple spheres. With frequent trips between U.S. cities and Europe, they were doing just that.

They explained that just as there are scientific **formulas** that help solve problems in chemistry and physics, there are technological and anatomical formulas they invented to tailor clothing for people of all shapes and sizes. The inspiration to invent and patent such formulas grew out of a desire to solve the problem of finding jeans that fit black women. It is no secret that most black women are blessed with sultry buttocks, curvaceous hips and thick thighs. Although attractive, finding jeans that contour to such a combination has been a design challenge for decades. Ms. Val and Stacey deem it important to help women of all races understand that it is not our bodies, but the designs, that need altering. Thankfully, Ms. Val and Stacey solved our problem. Their formula-driven designs make clothes that fit real people.

After learning about the technicalities of inventions and

denim patents, my mom and I were treated to a first-class fitting by the stylish Ms. Val. We both insisted that we wore certain sizes, but Ms. Val completed a visual scan and humbly disagreed. We reluctantly tried on jeans that seemed too small. Voila, they fit perfectly. I traditionally wear 6/8 in jeans sold in major retail chains. During my fitting with Ms. Val, I learned my true body size is a 2/4. And in her jeans, my 2/4 body made me scream "*Hallelujah.*" Instantly, my self-confidence soared to new heights and I couldn't stop smiling if someone paid me. For all those who dread the *shopping, fitting-room experience*, I urge you to schedule a fitting with Ms. Val. No matter your shape or size, I guarantee perpetual smiles induced by self-confidence will emerge. My mom agrees.

No one has had more challenges finding clothing that fits than my mom, Dr. Brenda Peterson. Perfectly shaped, she always has to buy apparel 2 sizes larger than her actual size. A fitting with Ms. Val was years overdue. I held my breath until she gracefully appeared. Watching mom step out of the fitting room with a new pep in her step delighted my soul. When mom modeled her reduced sized jeans, we all exhaled - "Wow"!

Stacey then asked, "*What are you doing here? You should be in Hollywood. You both belong in Hollywood. What's holding you back?*" Stacey's prophecy and questions deeply resonated as people have iterated this message all our lives. Before either of us could respond, Ms. Val completed a quick body scan (of us in our fitted jeans) and remarked, "Beautiful. Let me share some tips on how you both can stay in shape and always feel as good as you look."

Taking her advice, Mom beefed up her exercise routine and I began to exercise again. Three months later, we went to Hollywood for a tailor-made experience wearing our tailor-made jeans and had the time of our lives.

Influence is a huge part of leadership. Just as Ms. Val and Stacey influenced my thoughts and actions, they are influencing the landscape of the fashion industry. Their research and development company, House of MADE, consists of multiple fashion lines including *Beautiful Liberations* and *B. Black*. With multiple U.S and international patents and manufacturing partnerships, the couple is positioned to tailor-make anything that applies to the human body. They have filed design patents in five countries with a population mass of 4.5 billion people.

This power couple serves as proof that God is able to do *"exceeding abundantly above all that we ask or think, according to the power that worketh in us"* (Ephesians 3:20). Furthermore, they are working on a platform for Intelligence Tailoring and Visualization through the creation of their 3-D human body scanner designed to collect data and provide perfect sizing and measurements of the body in a matter seconds. This is tailor-made leadership on an unparalleled scale.

Like Ms. Val, I understand the pertinence and value of designing experiences that meet the needs of people. We both appreciate the fact that in most cases, one size does not fit all. Just as each person is unique, so are each person's life and work experiences.

In my early years as a coach and mentor, I quickly learned to gauge the self-interests of every school administrator and leader under my tutelage. Each had different strengths, areas for improvement and aspirations. Understanding them helped me to customize my coaching and tailor our work plans. What resulted was a group of individuals who blossomed into confident, courageous leaders consistently excelling in both administration and operations. My administrators and teacher leaders in turn worked with their teams to tailor learning experiences to meet the diverse learning needs of all students.

The sustainability of this powerful approach flies in the face of the *one size fits all* approach. Every great leader uses this approach to lead their lives and positively impact the lives of others. Ms. Val and I are living proof. It is evident that God tailor-made our lives to bring about His purpose on earth.

What has He called you to do? Who has He called you to lead? What have you tailor-made lately?

For the Spirit God gave us does not make us timid, but gives us power, love and self-discipline.
(2 Timothy 1:7)

Attribute 16
Leaderized Leadership
Lady Hendro Masenya

She walks in humility, stands with lions, sits among Kings, raises Princes, leads women, and supports the Bishop. Brilliance marks her beauty and the oil of gladness exudes from her captivating smile. In her presence, others are unleashed to be their best beautiful selves. At first glance, she bears the likeness of a trendy celebrity – fresh, vibrant, and stylish. Everyone relishes the opportunity to be a direct recipient of her radiance and stand in the space of her glow. What an honor to know Lady Hendro.

As we sat marveling at the exquisite artwork decorating the walls of the South African restaurant in downtown Pretoria, I kept trying to imagine her physical appearance and the manner of conversation in which we would engage. I wondered how she liked to spend her time and most importantly, her regimen for caring for herself, her family and her husband Bishop Thabo Masenya. After all, she is the woman handpicked by God to support one of the most powerful Prophets and Bishops on earth. Trust me; if you are a powerful Prophet in Africa, you are unquestionably one of the most powerful Prophets on earth.

At last, the wait was over. Upon entry, her tantalizing voice preceded her perfect frame. Even those who did not know her gawked when she entered the restaurant. She was more than I expected. During her waltz toward our table, I noticed her sway, her fragrance, her smile, her swag. Yes, "First Ladies" have the coolest swag (<u>S</u>ophistication <u>W</u>rought by <u>A</u>mazing <u>G</u>race). Wearing a distinctive turquoise pant outfit with matching leather purse and shoes, she could grace the cover of any international magazine. There was one thing missing: Arrogance. Aye, missing was the essence of arrogance that often surrounds women of her stature. By way of the spirit, I knew she was a woman of humility and love with the strength of a lioness. Halfway through lunch, she confirmed it.

Lady Hendro conversed with our ministry team (Apostle Abercrombie, Prophetess Sherrice, Brother Jerrell and I) as if we were time-honored friends. She shared the occurrences of her morning, including her conversation with her sons before school and business details she aimed to finalize. Yes, although she serves 72 churches alongside Bishop and cares for her family, she is an entrepreneur. I sometimes have a tough time wrangling my husband, ministry responsibilities and work, so I had to intrude a little to understand how she leads a balanced life. Since good leaders ask great questions, I politely dove in. Lady Hendro smiled at each delicately, probing question and provided simple responses in a matter-of-fact manner. Then Bishop interjected, offering a jaw-dropping comment. He told us that he taught his sons to stand before lions. We were all flabbergasted! Even my Pastor, who loves everything about lions, stared at Bishop in sheer astonishment. Did he just say he taught his sons how to stand before un-caged lions — as in the Kings of the Jungle? It has been stated that our relatives in Africa have an unmatched strength, but obviously rendezvousing with lions never entered my imagination.

Lady Hendro's response was just as jarring as our shocked faces. She chuckled and said, "It's a great experience," revealing that she too has stood before un-caged lions. I have been called a thrill-seeker on occasion and even took up the challenge to hold lion cubs while in South Africa, but honestly, I have not reached this level of being unleashed and unafraid.

When asked how to stand before lions and where one gets the courage, Lady Hendro boldly stated, "It's easy as long as you don't move, even if the lion roars." She shared that once you know what to do and use wisdom in executing; you will always be victorious, even over the King of the Jungle. She was teaching a revelatory lesson not often found in books. Powerful! This registered as one of my most intriguing lunch dates.

In less than an hour, I became the recipient of a leadership lesson I shall refer to as "Leaderized." From the moment Lady Hendro began to speak, I was *mesmerized, revitalized,* and *galvanized* through a series of *conceptualized* images that *neutralized* fearful thoughts that had unknowingly *crystallized* in my head preventing me from *capitalizing* on great opportunities and *maximizing* my full potential.

Basically, Exodus 14:13 came to life: *"Stand still and see the salvation of the Lord, which he will shew you today."* Just think, I had to travel to South Africa to get the full revelation of this scripture and understand how it applies to life. The salvation or rescue of the Lord coalesced with the use of wisdom are surely needed in a modern day "Daniel in the lion's den" experience. Like Daniel, Lady Hendro displayed total faith in God and lives to share this and similar experiences to help galvanize women to overcome fear with faith in order to seize opportunities and transform our worlds and the world at large. Even when the "lions" of life roar, we must stand firm, walk boldly, and take dominion over every area of our lives. This is how one Leaderizes!

I learned many valuable lessons in leadership from observing Lady Hendro. She not only successfully steers the reins of her own life through the guidance of the Holy Spirit, she models for other women how to steer their reigns in a balanced fashion.

Throughout the week, she (and Bishop) delegated our wrangling to those they trusted most: the Protocol Team. Lady Hendro and the Protocol team never missed a beat. They operated in excellence, love and humility. No ask was too great or outlandish. We even requested to be chauffeured to Lion's Park in celebration of our Pastor's birthday, which was at least an hour's drive in each direction. Lady Hendro ensured that we had the best tour guide, tickets, and personal photographer. Each Protocol team member epitomized servant leadership at its finest and is worthy of bearing the title Unleashed And Unafraid. I suppose they have come to exhibit such behavior because they appreciate the unconditional love, guidance, opportunities and support bestowed by Bishop Thabo and Lady Hendro Masenya.

My last hours spent with Lady Hendro on my first experience in South Africa were precious and priceless. We attended a fiery service where Bishop Masenya preached about Saul being focused on finding his family's donkeys (wealth). That message was definitely for me. His overarching lesson was: "Let nothing distract you from your God assignments."

Following the service, we fellowshipped over lunch at a complex complete with an upscale hotel, BB gun shooting range, and lush flower gardens. Lady Hendro shared words of wisdom, allowing us to get a deeper insight into her heart. A Mother of 72 churches, her heart beats for the salvation and progression of people. Following lunch, we toured an indigenous area. Lady Hendro educated us on the political and social structures of the area and their impact on the lives of the people. In a concerned tone, she discussed her and Bishop's strategic work to empower people spiritually and economically through evangelism and education. She even took us to a place where people and zebra co-exist. Clearly, she is the queen of her world, gracefully ruling from a place of strength and modesty.

It is no secret that the role of the "First Lady" shoulders levels of intricacies that some women would by-pass if given the choice. Many women who embrace their role as "First Lady" understand that leading their own lives is essential to avoid getting buried under the mounds of problems and paperwork associated with operating ministries. They are people too and we must all pause and remember that.

Lady Hendro makes this role look attractive. In service, she is a leading lady who actively participates in all aspects of service. Onlookers observe her freely worshipping, greeting parishioners and genuinely encouraging others. Perceptibly, her ability to lead her life "outside of the church" provides the refreshment she needs to continue to care for those "inside the church." She epitomizes Leaderizing by exercising balanced leadership, putting each aspect of life in its proper perspective.

Like Lady Hendro, we must all learn to *lead* our lives intentionally. Reflectively speaking, being unleashed and unafraid to *lead* my own life materialized after the release of *Volume I*. I was undoubtedly unleashed and unafraid to *live* courageously and triumphantly, but staggered a bit at leading my life. My awareness forced a new intentionality and the fruit resulted in my first Unleashed And Unafraid Conference, first trip to Nigeria and South Africa and the penning of *Unleashed And Unafraid Volume II*.

In other words, I have learned to stand before lions without moving even if they roar (figuratively speaking). I understand that until one can truly lead her life, despite opposition, rejection, criticism and the suppositions of those closest to her, one can never maximize her full potential and lead the life God intended her to live.

There are seven basic principles that Lady Hendro and I adhere to which allow us to successfully lead our own lives. This is not an exhaustive list and all principles should be applied with daily practice. Should you follow these, you will realize greater success in your own life:

1. Exercise great faith and know that with God nothing is impossible.
2. Serve others willingly, humbly and lovingly (all great leaders are great servants and the returns outweigh your service).
3. Understand your strengths and take the courage to monetize them (use your gifts and talents and start your own business if that's what's in your heart).
4. Think big and stay focused (don't shy away from challenges; turn them into opportunities).
5. Rid your life of unfruitful relationships and harsh critics who downplay your creativity (many do not have the capacity to understand your vision and will only hold you back).
6. Face life head-on, following proven patterns and instructions.
7. Use wisdom (intentionally apply key learning to enhance your life; never stop growing and pressing forward).

One must intentionally Leaderize her life in respectable ways that precede and follow her. Such "Leaderizing" must be done with real humility, authenticity and love.

This makes it easier to sustain one's own leadership and carve a path for others to follow. Lady Hendro and I are living proof.

What about you? It is your time. Leaderize!

About Dr. Sabrena Davis

Dr. Sabrena Davis is an author, speaker, minister, educator and coach. The owner at DSD Consultants, LLC, Dr. Sabrena is recognized as a woman of great distinction in the areas of education, leadership, spirituality, youth empowerment, and women's personal and professional power. She has a proven track record as a transformational leader who gets results. She has served in many capacities including Consultant, School Turnaround Expert, Superintendent, Principal Leadership Coach and Mentor, Conference Speaker and Facilitator, and Minister of Education. She has successfully trained, coached and mentored Principals and leaders in schools, churches and non-profit organizations who have realized exponential growth both personally and professionally.

Dr. Sabrena holds a Doctor of Education degree (EdD) from Newburgh Theological Seminary and Bible College (Indiana) and studied Educational Leadership at University of Illinois – Chicago. She earned her Master of Public Administration (MPA) from Troy University (Alabama) and Bachelor of Arts (BA) in English & Education from Dominican University (River Forest, Illinois).

She is the proud author of the acclaimed books, *Unleashed And Unafraid: Everyday Women of Excellence Who Live Intentionally Courageous Triumphant Lives* and *Unleashed And Unafraid: Courageous Women Transforming Generations Through the Excellence of Leadership*.

Unleashed And Unafraid is a game changer for women, as engagers are experiencing personal transformation on multiple levels. Dr. Sabrena has received many education and community awards for her work in leadership, including the Industry Buzzz Educator Award, The Golden Rose of Charity, Lincoln Laureate, African-American Heritage Award, and Outstanding Educator Award at a Blue Ribbon School of Excellence. Most recently, a book scholarship was named in her honor at the historic Theodore Roosevelt & Career Academy in Gary, Indiana. The Dr. Sabrena Davis Book Scholarship is awarded annually to assist students in paying tuition and/or book fees.

Thank you and continued blessings to my awesome
Unleashed And Unafraid Book Sponsor:

PANISH SHEA & BOYLE LLP

Author Contact Information

Dr. Sabrena Davis is available for Keynote Speaking, Presentations, Small Group Sessions, Book Club Engagements, Commencements, Conferences, Seminars, Webinars, Education and Community Meetings, Parent Meetings and radio and television interviews. For more information, contact her at

www.DrSabrenaDavis.com

Future Books and Products

You can look forward to the future writings of Dr. Sabrena Davis as she continues with a series of manuscripts outlining the courageous, triumphant lives of additional women, men and youth of distinction.

Unleashed And Unafraid Volume II

This book is available at **www.drsabrenadavis.com**, AmazonKindle as well as Amazon for the paperback book. Invest in you and your loved ones' futures today with the purchase of **Unleashed and Unafraid**!

www.ingramcontent.com/pod-product-compliance
Lightning Source LLC
Chambersburg PA
CBHW060813050426
42449CB00008B/1645